Mastering ChatGPT-5

Understanding, Applying, and Innovating with AI Conversations

By

Dr. Hesham Mohamed Elsherif

About the Author

Dr. Hesham Mohamed Elsherif stands at the forefront of library management, research, and the practical implementation of Artificial Intelligence (AI) in educational and library systems. With over 22 years of dedicated service in the field, he brings a wealth of expertise that bridges the worlds of technology, organizational leadership, and scholarship.

Dr. Elsherif's academic credentials are as diverse as they are impressive. He holds two doctoral degrees - one in **Management and Organizational Leadership** and the other in **Information Systems and Technology**. This dual specialization has equipped him with a holistic perspective on how institutions can effectively integrate emerging technologies, particularly AI, to optimize resource allocation, streamline operational processes, and enrich learning experiences.

A recognized authority in **empirical research methodology**, Dr. Elsherif specializes in **qualitative approaches** and **action research**. His mastery of these methodologies has not only bolstered his own scholarly work but has also allowed him to pioneer new ways of investigating and implementing AI-driven solutions in school, academic, and public libraries. Whether he is designing user-centric AI tools or conducting in-depth studies on technology adoption, Dr. Elsherif's methodical and data-driven approach consistently yields impactful, real-world results.

Over the years, he has made significant strides in shaping the academic community - not just as a **professional researcher**, but also as an **Adjunct Professor**. In the classroom, Dr. Elsherif has a remarkable ability to translate complex theories into accessible insights, thereby training a new generation of thought leaders and specialists in both library science and technology. This multifaceted role, spanning teaching, research, and practice, has cemented his status as a **pioneer** whose influence extends well beyond traditional academic boundaries.

Dr. Elsherif's expertise and passion are truly global in scope. He has served as a **consultant to numerous educational institutions worldwide**, offering guidance on best practices, AI integration strategies, and effective management models. His international collaborations speak to the versatility of his knowledge, which is informed by a deep understanding of how AI can enhance resource discovery, user engagement, and scholarly communication across cultural and institutional contexts.

Central to Dr. Elsherif's mission is the belief that **innovative technologies**, including AI, must be harnessed responsibly and ethically. This commitment is evident in his approach to library management and educational technology, where he advocates for solutions that are inclusive, data-secure, and aligned with the core values of academic freedom and public service. By focusing on ethical implementation, he ensures that advancements in AI serve learners, educators, and researchers effectively and fairly.

Today, Dr. Elsherif continues to break new ground in **library innovation**, **academic research**, and **technology leadership**. Combining a passion for education with an unparalleled depth of knowledge, he remains a guiding force - **inspiring, educating, and leading** in library systems, educational institutions, and beyond. Through his work, he illuminates the path toward a future where AI seamlessly complements human expertise, thereby enriching the academic and public spheres for generations to come.

Preface

When artificial intelligence began to step out of research labs and into our daily lives, many of us saw it as a distant curiosity. Then, in just a few short years, conversational AI evolved from clunky chatbots into a technology capable of nuanced, human-like dialogue. With the arrival of ChatGPT-5, that leap feels even more profound. This is no longer a tool that simply answers questions. It is a partner in thinking, a collaborator in creativity, and in many cases, a catalyst for innovation.

Yet, for all its potential, ChatGPT-5 can feel like a vast ocean. Many approach it with excitement, only to discover that without guidance, it is easy to get lost in shallow waters or swept into currents of misinformation, bias, or unrealistic expectations. The purpose of this book is to be your map and compass. It aims to explain not only *what* ChatGPT-5 can do but *how* it works, *why* it behaves the way it does, and *where* it can take you if used thoughtfully.

This is not a collection of magic prompts or secret tricks. Instead, it is a guided exploration - part technical manual, part field guide, part ethical handbook. Whether you are an educator looking to transform your classroom, a business leader seeking efficiency, a developer integrating AI into your software, or simply a curious mind eager to understand the forces shaping our digital future, you will find tools, examples, and insights here to help you master this new medium of communication.

Above all, this book is about empowerment. AI is not here to replace human imagination or judgment. It is here to extend them. My hope is that by the final chapter, you will not only understand ChatGPT-5 in detail but will also feel confident in weaving it into your own work, projects, and ideas - responsibly, creatively, and with a sense of possibility.

The future of human-AI collaboration is not something we must wait for. It is already here. Let us explore it together.

Who Should Read This Book?

This book is for anyone who wants to move beyond curiosity and truly understand how to work with ChatGPT-5. While its applications span almost every industry and field, you will find it especially valuable if you belong to one of the following groups:

1. **Educators and Trainers**
   If you teach, coach, or design learning materials, this book will show you how to use ChatGPT-5 to create lessons, explain complex topics, and provide personalized feedback.

2. **Business Leaders and Entrepreneurs**
   From automating customer service to generating strategic ideas, ChatGPT-5 can transform workflows. You will learn practical ways to integrate it into your operations and decision-making.

3. **Writers and Creatives**
   Authors, screenwriters, journalists, marketers, and content creators will discover how ChatGPT-5 can spark ideas, refine drafts, and support every stage of the creative process.

4. **Researchers and Analysts**
   If your work involves gathering, analyzing, and synthesizing information, this book will help you leverage ChatGPT-5 for faster research and clearer insights—while avoiding common pitfalls.

5. **Students and Lifelong Learners**
   Whether you are studying for exams, exploring new subjects, or pursuing hobbies, you will find techniques to make ChatGPT-5 a personalized tutor and study partner.

6. **Developers and Technologists**
   If you want to build apps, automate tasks, or integrate AI into

software, the technical chapters will give you the foundational knowledge and coding approaches you need.

7. **Professionals Seeking Efficiency**
   Lawyers, consultants, project managers, and other specialists will learn how to streamline reports, draft documents, and prepare presentations in collaboration with ChatGPT-5.

8. **Anyone Curious About the Future of AI**
   If you simply want to understand where AI is headed and how it can fit into your personal or professional life, this book will give you both the big picture and the fine details.

You do not need a background in programming or artificial intelligence to benefit from this book. All technical concepts are explained clearly, and real-world examples are provided throughout. What you do need is an open mind, a willingness to experiment, and a desire to explore the possibilities of human-AI collaboration.

How to Use This Book

This book is designed to be both a learning resource and a practical guide. You can read it cover to cover for a full understanding of ChatGPT-5 or dip into the chapters most relevant to your goals.

1. Choose Your Path

- **If you are new to AI** start with *Part I: Foundations of ChatGPT-5*. These chapters explain how the model works, its history, and its limitations in plain language.
- **If you want to get productive fast** begin with *Part II: Practical Usage and Techniques*. You will find step-by-step guidance, examples, and prompt strategies you can try immediately.
- **If you have a specific field in mind** explore *Part III: Specialized Applications* to see how ChatGPT-5 can be applied in business, education, creative work, research, and more.

2. Practice as You Read

Throughout the book, you will find exercises, prompt challenges, and real-world scenarios. These are not optional extras - they are your best opportunity to develop skill through hands-on experience. Keep a ChatGPT-5 session open while you read so you can test ideas instantly.

3. Learn in Layers

Concepts are introduced at a beginner-friendly level and then expanded into more advanced techniques. If something feels too complex at first, you can return to it after trying the basics.

4. Use the Templates and Tools

Appendix A contains ready-made prompts and frameworks you can adapt to your own projects. Treat them as starting points rather than final answers - your own context will shape the best results.

5. Keep Ethics in Mind
The chapters on safety, fairness, and responsible use are just as important as the technical sections. Using ChatGPT-5 well means using it with awareness of its risks and impact.

6. Return for Reference
Once you have read the book, it can serve as a quick-reference manual. The index and glossary will help you locate specific concepts, and the appendices keep key resources at your fingertips.

You do not need to be an AI expert to benefit from this book, but you will get the most from it if you approach it with curiosity, patience, and a willingness to experiment. Treat ChatGPT-5 not as a shortcut to answers but as a collaborative tool - and you will find that your skills grow along with your understanding.

Table of Contents

Introduction

Artificial intelligence has been a subject of fascination for decades, but in recent years it has moved from science fiction into our daily reality. AI no longer hides in research labs or powers only specialized applications. It now sits on our desktops, in our phones, and even in our homes - ready to hold conversations, answer questions, and collaborate on projects.

ChatGPT-5 is a milestone in this shift. It is not simply a faster or bigger version of what came before. It represents a leap in conversational depth, context awareness, and adaptability. It can read and respond to text, analyze images, generate ideas, assist with research, guide learning, and adapt to a wide variety of styles and purposes. It is multimodal, meaning it can work across different types of input and output, opening new possibilities for interaction.

But here's the challenge: the difference between using ChatGPT-5 casually and using it effectively is vast. A casual user might ask for a simple answer and get something useful. An informed user can design prompts, structure interactions, and integrate the system into their workflows in ways that transform how they work, learn, and create. This book is about helping you become that informed user.

You will not find hype here, nor will you find vague promises of "AI magic." Instead, you will get a grounded, clear, and practical exploration of what ChatGPT-5 is, how it works, what it can and cannot do, and how to apply it thoughtfully in real contexts. We will cover the fundamentals of large language models, the art and science of prompt engineering, and advanced strategies for specialized use cases - from business and education to research and creative work.

The book is organized into five main parts. First, we explore the **foundations** of ChatGPT-5 - its evolution, inner workings, and the ethical considerations of using such a system. Then we move into

practical usage and techniques, where you will learn how to interact with the model effectively. From there, we examine **specialized applications** that show ChatGPT-5 in action across different industries. We then turn to **challenges, risks, and the future**, equipping you to navigate AI with critical thinking. Finally, the **practice and mastery** section provides exercises, templates, and real-world case studies to help you sharpen your skills.

Throughout the book, you will find examples you can test immediately, prompts you can adapt to your own work, and exercises to build your confidence. You will also see discussions of limitations, biases, and ethical questions - because mastering ChatGPT-5 is not just about knowing what to ask, but also knowing when to question the answers.

The future of human-AI interaction is not a distant horizon; it is already unfolding. Whether you want to enhance your productivity, expand your creative toolkit, or better understand the forces shaping our digital age, this book is your companion in that journey. By the time you finish, you will not only know how to use ChatGPT-5 - you will know how to think with it, challenge it, and collaborate with it in ways that are both powerful and responsible.

Part I: Foundations of ChatGPT-5

Chapter 1 – The Evolution of AI Conversational Models

From Early Chatbots to ChatGPT-5

The journey from the first conversational programs to ChatGPT-5 is a story of technological persistence, creative problem solving, and steadily increasing sophistication in how machines understand and generate human language.

The earliest chatbots appeared in the 1960s and 1970s. One of the most famous was ELIZA, developed by Joseph Weizenbaum at the Massachusetts Institute of Technology. ELIZA simulated a Rogerian psychotherapist, responding with generic prompts such as "Tell me more about that" or "How do you feel about it." While its responses were simple pattern matches, ELIZA demonstrated that even limited programs could give an illusion of conversation when carefully designed.

In the 1980s and 1990s, chatbots like PARRY and ALICE expanded the idea. PARRY attempted to mimic the conversational patterns of a person with paranoid schizophrenia. ALICE, short for Artificial Linguistic Internet Computer Entity, used a large set of manually written rules and patterns to create more varied conversations. These systems relied entirely on scripted interactions and could not truly learn from new data, but they set the foundation for how humans might interact with computers in natural language.

The early 2000s brought more advanced statistical methods and the first signs of machine learning applied to language. Chatbots began using probabilistic models that could choose responses based on statistical likelihood rather than fixed scripts. However, these models still lacked deep contextual understanding and often produced irrelevant or repetitive answers.

A major turning point came with the introduction of deep learning in the 2010s. Neural networks, particularly recurrent neural networks

(RNNs) and later transformers, allowed models to process sequences of text with far greater context awareness. In 2017, researchers at Google introduced the transformer architecture in a paper titled "Attention Is All You Need." This design became the backbone of modern large language models because it could handle long-range dependencies and capture meaning in a way that older methods could not.

OpenAI entered the scene with the Generative Pretrained Transformer (GPT) series. GPT-1 showed that training on large amounts of text could produce a model that generated coherent sentences. GPT-2, released in 2019, surprised many with its ability to produce paragraphs of readable, contextually relevant text. GPT-3 scaled this idea dramatically, with 175 billion parameters, making it capable of a wide range of tasks without additional training. GPT-4 further improved reasoning ability, reduced errors, and expanded its capabilities across languages and domains.

ChatGPT-5 represents another significant step forward. It retains the scale and adaptability of earlier versions but introduces enhanced multimodal capabilities, allowing it to process and generate not only text but also images, code, and in some implementations, audio. It has a deeper understanding of context over extended conversations and can shift smoothly between topics without losing track of the user's intent. It is also better aligned with human values through reinforcement learning from human feedback, making its outputs more helpful, accurate, and safe.

This evolution from early rule-based chatbots to a highly capable, context-aware, and multimodal system reflects the broader history of artificial intelligence. Each stage built on the successes and limitations of the previous one, moving closer to the vision of a conversational partner that can genuinely assist, inform, and collaborate with people in a natural way. ChatGPT-5 is not the final destination in this journey, but it is one of the most advanced milestones to date.

Key Milestones: GPT-1 through GPT-5

The development of the GPT series by OpenAI marks one of the most significant progressions in artificial intelligence. Each generation built on the achievements of the previous one, introducing new capabilities, larger models, and improved alignment with human communication. Understanding these milestones helps explain why ChatGPT-5 is such an advanced tool today.

GPT-1: The Proof of Concept (2018)

GPT-1 was the starting point of the Generative Pretrained Transformer series. With 117 million parameters, it demonstrated that a language model could be trained on large amounts of publicly available text and then fine-tuned for specific tasks. The model used the transformer architecture introduced by Google in 2017, which allowed it to understand relationships between words over long distances in text. Although its performance was modest compared to later versions, GPT-1 proved that a single model could adapt to different language tasks without being retrained from scratch.

GPT-2: Scaling Up and Surprising the World (2019)

GPT-2 expanded the architecture to 1.5 billion parameters, significantly improving fluency and coherence in generated text. It could write full paragraphs that often felt human-written, handle a wide variety of topics, and adapt its style to different prompts. GPT-2 attracted global attention because of concerns about misuse, which initially led OpenAI to delay the full release. It became a clear sign that scaling up model size could lead to dramatic improvements in quality.

GPT-3: General-Purpose AI Text Generation (2020)

GPT-3 marked a massive leap in scale, with 175 billion parameters. This size enabled it to perform tasks it had never been explicitly trained for, such as writing code, generating poetry, explaining concepts, and even solving some reasoning problems. GPT-3 introduced the idea of "few-shot" and "zero-shot" learning, where the model could perform a task based on minimal or no examples in the prompt. It quickly became the foundation for a wide range of applications and services, including the early versions of ChatGPT.

GPT-4: Reasoning, Accuracy, and Multimodality (2023)
GPT-4 brought significant improvements in reasoning ability, factual accuracy, and safety. It handled complex multi-step instructions more reliably and reduced the rate of hallucinations compared to GPT-3. GPT-4 also introduced multimodal capabilities, meaning it could process both text and images in some versions. This made it useful for interpreting diagrams, analyzing photographs, and providing more contextually rich responses. The model's alignment with human feedback improved, making it more reliable for professional and educational use.

GPT-5: Contextual Depth, Adaptability, and Expanded Multimodality (2025)
ChatGPT-5 builds on the strengths of GPT-4 while addressing its limitations. It can maintain context over much longer conversations, follow nuanced instructions with greater accuracy, and switch between topics without losing the thread of the discussion. Its multimodal features are more deeply integrated, enabling seamless interaction with text, images, and in some cases audio or video. GPT-5 is also better at customizing its style and tone to match the user's needs, making it more versatile for both personal and professional applications. Safety and alignment measures have been further refined to reduce bias and provide outputs that are more helpful and ethically responsible.

From GPT-1's modest beginnings to GPT-5's sophisticated, multimodal capabilities, the series demonstrates the power of iterative innovation. Each version did not simply grow in size but evolved in its ability to understand context, reason through complex instructions, and collaborate effectively with human users. GPT-5 stands as a milestone in this ongoing journey, pointing toward even more advanced AI systems in the future.

How LLM Changed Communication

The arrival of large language models, or LLMs, has altered the way people create, share, and interpret information. These models, trained on vast amounts of text from books, articles, websites, and other sources, can generate human-like responses to written prompts. Their influence has extended far beyond academic research into everyday life, affecting business, education, creativity, and personal interaction.

One of the most profound changes has been the speed and scale of communication. Before LLMs, tasks such as drafting detailed reports, summarizing long documents, or translating complex text into simpler language required significant human effort and time. With LLMs like ChatGPT-5, these tasks can now be completed in seconds. This has allowed individuals and organizations to process and respond to information far more quickly, enabling faster decision-making and more agile workflows.

LLMs have also reshaped the accessibility of information. People who may not have specialized knowledge in a subject can ask an LLM for clear explanations, tailored to their level of understanding. This has reduced barriers to entry for learning new skills or exploring unfamiliar fields. It has also opened new possibilities for inclusive communication, with LLMs able to translate between languages or adapt content for different literacy levels.

Another major change is in personalization. Large language models can adapt their responses to match a specific tone, style, or perspective. This means communication can be tailored to suit different audiences, whether for professional correspondence, educational materials, marketing content, or casual conversation. The result is a more dynamic and flexible approach to message delivery that was not possible with traditional automated systems.

Collaboration has also been transformed. LLMs can serve as idea generators, co-writers, or brainstorming partners. They can suggest structures for presentations, refine drafts, or provide alternative perspectives during problem-solving. This capability has made them valuable in creative industries, research teams, and even personal projects, where a steady flow of ideas can accelerate progress and innovation.

However, these benefits come with new responsibilities. Because LLMs can generate convincing but incorrect or biased information, users must apply critical thinking and verify important facts. This has shifted part of the communication process toward evaluating and curating AI-generated content. In this sense, the role of the human communicator has evolved from solely creating messages to also guiding, refining, and validating them.

Ultimately, LLMs have not simply made communication faster or easier. They have introduced a new model of interaction where humans and machines collaborate in producing, interpreting, and sharing information. This partnership has the potential to make communication more efficient, inclusive, and creative, but it also demands careful use to ensure accuracy, fairness, and ethical responsibility.

Chapter 2 – Inside the Mind of ChatGPT-5

What a Transformer Model Is

The transformer model is the core architecture that powers ChatGPT-5. It is a type of neural network that specializes in processing sequences of data, such as sentences or paragraphs, in a way that captures both local and global context. Introduced in 2017 by researchers at Google in the paper "Attention Is All You Need," the transformer replaced older sequence-processing methods like recurrent neural networks (RNNs) and long short-term memory networks (LSTMs).

What makes the transformer revolutionary is its use of an attention mechanism. In earlier models, the processing of a sentence often happened step-by-step, which made it difficult for the system to remember distant words and relationships. Transformers take a different approach. They look at the entire sequence of words at once and determine how much each word should "pay attention" to every other word. This allows the model to understand relationships across long distances in text with much greater efficiency.

In a transformer, the main building blocks are:

1. **Embedding Layer** - This converts words into numerical representations called vectors. Each vector contains information about the meaning of the word and its relationships to other words.

2. **Encoder and Decoder Layers** - The encoder reads and processes the input text, while the decoder generates the output text. In models like ChatGPT, these two functions are often integrated since the system is both reading and generating language in the same framework.

3. **Attention Mechanism** - This is the heart of the transformer. It calculates scores that show how relevant each word in a sequence is to every other word. This allows the model to give more weight to important words when forming its understanding of the text.

4. **Feed-Forward Networks** - After the attention step, the information flows through fully connected layers that further refine the representation of the text.

5. **Positional Encoding** - Since transformers process all words in parallel, they need a way to remember word order. Positional encoding assigns each word a location-based value so the model can reconstruct the sequence meaning.

Because of this architecture, transformers can be scaled up to very large sizes without losing their ability to track complex patterns in language. ChatGPT-5 is built on an extremely large transformer model, containing billions of parameters. These parameters store learned information about language structure, facts, reasoning patterns, and stylistic nuances.

Tokenization and Context Windows

Before ChatGPT-5 can process text, it must convert that text into a form it can understand mathematically. This process is called **tokenization**. A token is a small unit of text that can represent a whole word, part of a word, or even punctuation. The exact size of a token depends on the model's tokenizer, which is the set of rules that decides how text is split.

For example, the sentence:
"ChatGPT is powerful."
might be broken into tokens like:
["Chat", "G", "PT", " is", " powerful", "."]

Each of these tokens is then converted into a unique numerical ID, which the model uses as input for further processing. These IDs are transformed into vectors during the embedding stage so the model can work with them in a multidimensional mathematical space.

Tokenization is necessary because large language models do not operate directly on raw text. Instead, they work with sequences of numbers that represent both the meaning and relationships of the text.

Context Windows

The **context window** defines how much text the model can consider at one time. It is measured in tokens, not characters or words. If ChatGPT-5 has a context window of 32,000 tokens, that means it can "see" and use that many tokens from both the prompt and its own previous responses combined.

A larger context window allows for longer conversations, more detailed instructions, and better handling of documents or transcripts without losing track of earlier information. However, once the limit is reached, the oldest tokens are dropped from the active memory of the model. This is similar to how a person might forget the earliest parts of a very long conversation if too much new information is introduced.

ChatGPT-5 uses its context window to maintain coherence. It looks back at previous tokens to decide how to respond, weighing their importance through the attention mechanism in its transformer architecture. This is why well-structured prompts and clear context can dramatically improve the quality of responses.

Key Points

- Tokenization breaks text into small units that can be processed numerically.

- The context window sets the maximum number of tokens the model can use in a single interaction.
- Longer context windows enable more detailed and coherent multi-turn conversations.
- Once the window is full, older information is dropped and cannot be referenced directly.

Multimodal Capabilities (Text, Image, Audio)

One of the most significant advancements in ChatGPT-5 is its ability to operate as a truly multimodal system. Earlier language models primarily worked with text. While they could generate high-quality written responses, they could not directly process other forms of input such as images or audio. ChatGPT-5 changes this by integrating multiple types of data into a single unified framework.

Text Processing

Text remains the core strength of ChatGPT-5. It can interpret natural language prompts, analyze documents, summarize articles, translate between languages, and generate creative or technical content. Its improvements in contextual awareness mean it can maintain accuracy and coherence across longer conversations, even when topics shift or become complex.

Image Understanding and Generation

ChatGPT-5 can analyze images alongside text, allowing it to perform tasks such as describing visual scenes, identifying objects, interpreting charts, or extracting information from photos of documents. It can also collaborate with image generation models to create realistic or artistic visuals based on textual prompts. This integration of vision and language enables richer, more context-aware responses, such as explaining a photograph and then generating related text or graphics.

Audio Processing

With audio capabilities, ChatGPT-5 can transcribe speech into text, respond to spoken questions, and even analyze audio content for tone, emotion, or meaning. In certain implementations, it can produce spoken output, making it suitable for interactive voice assistants, accessibility tools, and language learning applications. The ability to process audio means users can interact naturally without needing to type, and the system can adapt to different accents, speech speeds, and conversational styles.

Why Multimodality Matters

Multimodal capability allows ChatGPT-5 to understand and respond in ways that are closer to human communication, which often combines words, visuals, and sounds. For example, a teacher could upload an image of a historical map, ask the model to explain its details, and then receive an audio summary suitable for students. A business analyst could feed the model a chart, request a written explanation, and follow up with spoken clarifications. This flexibility makes ChatGPT-5 more versatile and useful across diverse domains.

Integration Across Modes

The real power of ChatGPT-5's multimodality comes from its ability to blend these inputs and outputs seamlessly. It can take a text description and an image together to form a more accurate understanding. It can listen to an audio file, transcribe it, and then analyze the content in written form. This cross-modal reasoning enables workflows that were not possible with earlier single-mode systems.

By incorporating text, image, and audio into a single processing pipeline, ChatGPT-5 moves closer to the vision of AI as a universal communication partner, capable of adapting to the medium that best suits the user's needs. This evolution is not simply an addition of features, but a transformation in how AI can participate in complex, human-like exchanges of information.

Differences from GPT-4

ChatGPT-5 builds on the foundation established by GPT-4 but introduces a range of technical and functional improvements that significantly enhance its capabilities. These changes are not only a matter of increased scale, but also of more refined architecture, improved alignment with human communication, and deeper integration of multimodal processing.

1. Expanded Context Window

One of the most noticeable upgrades is the size of the context window. GPT-4 could handle a substantial amount of tokens, but GPT-5 increases that limit even further. This means the model can remember and reference more of the ongoing conversation or larger input documents without losing earlier context. As a result, it maintains coherence over much longer interactions, making it better suited for tasks such as legal document review, lengthy research analysis, or book-length text generation.

2. More Advanced Multimodality

GPT-4 introduced the ability to process both text and images, but GPT-5 extends this to more seamlessly integrate text, images, and audio in a single interaction. For example, GPT-5 can analyze a photograph, listen to a spoken question about it, and then respond with both a written explanation and an audio answer. The system's multimodal reasoning is more fluid, allowing it to combine insights from different input types into a unified, context-aware output.

3. Improved Reasoning and Accuracy

While GPT-4 was already a strong reasoning model, GPT-5's training and architecture enhancements allow it to handle multi-step logical problems and nuanced queries with higher precision. It is better at following complex instructions, maintaining logical consistency, and producing outputs that align more closely with the intended meaning of the prompt. Its factual accuracy has also been improved through more advanced training data selection and fine-tuning processes.

4. More Customizable Responses
GPT-5 offers greater control over tone, style, and level of detail. Users can more effectively shape the personality and depth of responses, making it adaptable for professional, creative, or educational purposes. While GPT-4 could adjust style to some extent, GPT-5 is more responsive to subtle shifts in instruction, which allows for more precise tailoring of communication.

5. Better Long-Term Conversational Memory
In certain implementations, GPT-5 can maintain a form of extended memory across sessions, allowing it to remember preferences, previous tasks, and user-specific details for future interactions. GPT-4 lacked this capability in most configurations, requiring each conversation to start fresh. This improvement makes GPT-5 more useful for ongoing projects, tutoring, or personalized support.

6. Enhanced Safety and Bias Reduction
GPT-5 includes improved content filtering and alignment mechanisms. It is more effective at detecting and avoiding harmful, biased, or inappropriate outputs while still providing informative and helpful responses. These safeguards are the result of more rigorous human feedback loops and better fine-tuning during the training process.

7. Increased Efficiency in Processing
GPT-5's architecture has been optimized for faster and more efficient computation, which can lead to reduced latency and better scalability in high-demand environments. This is especially important for enterprise applications and real-time interactions.

In summary, GPT-5 surpasses GPT-4 not only in size and raw capacity but also in the depth of its multimodal integration, the sophistication of its reasoning abilities, the personalization of its responses, and the safety of its outputs. These improvements collectively make it a more versatile, accurate, and adaptable conversational AI.

Chapter 3 – Data, Training, and Knowledge

How GPT-5 Learns from Massive Datasets

GPT-5 is the result of a large-scale training process that involves feeding the model vast amounts of text, images, and other forms of data. The goal is to teach the system patterns in language, reasoning, and knowledge so it can generate coherent, contextually relevant, and accurate responses.

The process begins with **data collection**. This includes text from books, academic papers, websites, news articles, code repositories, and other publicly available or licensed sources. For multimodal capabilities, datasets also include images paired with descriptive text, as well as audio recordings with transcriptions. These diverse sources ensure that GPT-5 is exposed to a wide range of topics, writing styles, and formats.

Once collected, the data is **cleaned and preprocessed**. This step removes duplicates, filters out low-quality or irrelevant content, and standardizes formatting. The cleaning process is essential because the quality of the model's responses depends heavily on the quality of its training data. If the dataset contains too much misinformation or bias, the model is more likely to reflect those flaws.

The cleaned data is then converted into **tokens**, which are smaller units of text such as words, word parts, or punctuation marks. Tokens are transformed into numerical representations called embeddings, which allow the model to process them mathematically.

The **training phase** involves exposing the transformer architecture to these tokens in sequence. GPT-5 learns by predicting the next token based on the tokens it has already seen. Every time it predicts incorrectly, the system adjusts its internal parameters to reduce future errors. This is done through a process called backpropagation, where errors are measured and used to fine-tune the billions of parameters that make up the model.

A key factor in GPT-5's learning process is **scale**. The more parameters a model has, and the more diverse its training data, the better it can capture complex patterns and subtle relationships in language. GPT-5's vast size allows it to store a huge amount of learned associations, which makes it more versatile in handling different topics, tones, and tasks.

In addition to raw pretraining, GPT-5 undergoes **fine-tuning**. This is where the model is adjusted for safety, accuracy, and alignment with human expectations. Fine-tuning can include supervised learning with curated datasets and reinforcement learning from human feedback (RLHF). In RLHF, human reviewers rank model outputs for quality and correctness, and these rankings guide further training to make the system more useful and reliable.

While GPT-5 can process and generate information on an impressive scale, it does not "understand" the world in the way humans do. Its knowledge is a reflection of patterns found in its training data rather than personal experience or independent reasoning. However, the sheer size and diversity of its datasets allow it to approximate human-like reasoning and conversation in many contexts.

By learning from massive datasets, GPT-5 achieves a balance between broad general knowledge and the ability to adapt to specific requests. Its training process equips it to function as a highly capable language and multimodal model that can work across countless domains.

Fine-Tuning and Reinforcement Learning

While the initial pretraining of GPT-5 gives the model a broad understanding of language, it is the fine-tuning and RLHF stages that transform it into a practical, user-friendly, and safe tool. Pretraining teaches the model patterns in data, but it does not guarantee that it will respond in ways that are helpful, aligned with user intent, or free from harmful biases. Fine-tuning and RLHF bridge this gap by guiding the model toward higher quality outputs.

Fine-Tuning

Fine-tuning is the process of taking the pretrained model and adjusting it with additional, curated datasets. These datasets are chosen to reinforce desired behaviors and reduce unwanted ones. For example, fine-tuning can train the model to produce step-by-step explanations in problem solving, to use a professional tone in business contexts, or to avoid making unsafe suggestions.

Fine-tuning datasets can be domain-specific. If a company wants GPT-5 to act as a legal assistant, it might be fine-tuned on case law, contracts, and legal writing. This approach allows the general model to become highly specialized without losing its original broad knowledge. Fine-tuning also helps calibrate the model's style and tone so it is consistent with the intended audience.

Reinforcement Learning from Human Feedback (RLHF)

RLHF is a method that uses human evaluators to improve the model's performance. The process begins by generating multiple responses to the same prompt. Human reviewers then rank these responses according to quality, accuracy, safety, and alignment with the intended task. The model is updated to prefer the higher-ranked responses in future interactions.

This approach is especially important for tasks that involve subjective judgment or nuanced reasoning. For example, when a question can be answered in multiple valid ways, RLHF teaches the model to prefer the one that best matches the user's context and intent.

The RLHF Process

1. **Prompt Generation** – The model is given a set of prompts, often designed to test its abilities in reasoning, clarity, safety, and helpfulness.

2. **Response Sampling** – The model generates several candidate answers for each prompt.
3. **Human Ranking** – Trained reviewers compare the responses and rank them from best to worst.
4. **Reward Model Training** – A separate model learns to predict the rankings given by humans.
5. **Policy Optimization** – The main model is updated to produce outputs that score highly according to the reward model.

Benefits of Fine-Tuning and RLHF in GPT-5

- **Better Alignment**: GPT-5 becomes more likely to follow instructions exactly as intended.
- **Improved Safety**: Harmful, biased, or factually incorrect outputs are reduced.
- **Consistency**: Responses become more predictable in tone and format, which is valuable for professional use.
- **Adaptability**: The model can be customized for specific industries or user needs.

Through fine-tuning and RLHF, GPT-5 gains not only greater technical accuracy but also a more human-like ability to provide relevant, respectful, and context-aware responses. This combination ensures that GPT-5 is not just a large language model with raw power, but also a refined assistant capable of meeting real-world demands.

Limitations in Data Recency and Bias

Although GPT-5 represents one of the most advanced AI language models to date, it still faces limitations in both the freshness of its knowledge and the neutrality of its outputs. Understanding these constraints is essential for using the model effectively and responsibly.

Limitations in Data Recency

GPT-5's knowledge is based on the datasets it was trained on, which are collected up to a certain point in time. This means the model does not have an automatic connection to real-time information unless it is integrated with external tools or given updated data through fine-tuning. For example, if GPT-5's training data only extends to early 2025, it will not contain direct knowledge of events, publications, or developments that occur after that date.

As a result, GPT-5 may be unaware of the latest scientific discoveries, legal changes, or cultural trends. If asked about recent events outside its training range, it may respond with outdated information or make educated guesses based on prior patterns. This can be problematic for tasks where up-to-date accuracy is critical, such as financial forecasting or legal compliance.

Limitations in Bias

Bias in GPT-5 stems from the fact that it learns from large datasets containing human-generated content. All human writing reflects the perspectives, assumptions, and cultural norms of its authors. This means that the data can contain both subtle and explicit biases, which the model may reproduce in its responses.

Bias can manifest in different ways:

- **Cultural bias**: Certain ideas, idioms, or viewpoints may be overrepresented due to the dominance of specific languages or regions in the dataset.
- **Gender and demographic bias**: The model may unconsciously favor or stereotype certain groups based on patterns it has learned.

- **Topical bias**: Popular topics and mainstream viewpoints are often better represented than niche subjects or minority perspectives.

Why These Limitations Matter

Both data recency and bias influence the reliability and fairness of GPT-5's outputs. Outdated information can lead to incorrect conclusions, while biased responses can reinforce stereotypes or unintentionally marginalize certain voices.

Mitigation Strategies

While these limitations cannot be entirely removed, there are strategies to reduce their impact:

- Pair GPT-5 with real-time data retrieval tools to fill knowledge gaps.
- Use fact-checking to verify important information.
- Apply bias detection and correction frameworks in workflows that use GPT-5 for sensitive decisions.
- Provide the model with diverse and balanced prompts to encourage broader perspectives.

Recognizing these limitations allows users to treat GPT-5 not as an unquestionable authority but as a powerful assistant that must be guided, verified, and supplemented with additional sources. This awareness is key to ensuring that interactions with the model are both accurate and fair.

Chapter 4 – Ethics and Safety in AI Conversations

Bias and Fairness

Bias and fairness are central concerns in the ethical use of ChatGPT-5. Because the model is trained on massive datasets collected from human-created content, it inevitably inherits some of the biases present in those sources. These biases can influence how the model responds to prompts, the examples it uses, the perspectives it emphasizes, and the assumptions it makes.

Understanding Bias in AI

Bias in AI refers to systematic patterns of unfairness in how the model processes or presents information. In GPT-5, bias can appear in several ways:

- **Cultural Bias**: The model may give more weight to viewpoints, idioms, and values that are dominant in the cultures most represented in its training data.
- **Demographic Bias**: GPT-5 may unintentionally stereotype or favor certain genders, ethnic groups, or age ranges.
- **Topical Bias**: Popular or mainstream viewpoints on certain subjects may be better represented than niche or minority perspectives.
- **Confirmation Bias**: The model might generate responses that align too closely with the framing of the question, without challenging incorrect assumptions.

Why Fairness Matters

Unaddressed bias can reinforce harmful stereotypes, exclude marginalized perspectives, and limit the diversity of information users receive. This can affect trust in the model and undermine its value as a tool for education, decision-making, and communication. Fairness is not only an ethical responsibility but also a practical necessity for ensuring the model serves a broad and diverse audience effectively.

Mitigating Bias in GPT-5

Several strategies are used to reduce bias and improve fairness:

1. **Diverse Training Data**: Efforts are made to include multiple cultural, geographic, and demographic perspectives in the dataset.
2. **Bias Detection Tools**: Automated methods help identify patterns in model outputs that suggest unfair representation or stereotyping.
3. **Human Review**: Human evaluators assess outputs for fairness and provide feedback that is incorporated into reinforcement learning from human feedback (RLHF).
4. **User Controls**: Features that allow users to adjust tone, style, or perspective help balance responses according to user needs.

User Role in Ensuring Fairness

While OpenAI and other developers can reduce bias in the training process, users also have a role in promoting fairness. By asking clear, neutral, and well-structured questions, users can reduce the likelihood of inadvertently reinforcing biased outputs. Fact-checking responses and seeking information from multiple sources also help maintain balance and accuracy.

The Ongoing Challenge

Bias cannot be completely eliminated from AI because it is deeply rooted in human language and culture. However, it can be managed and reduced to create fairer, more inclusive interactions. In the case of GPT-5, continuous improvements in dataset selection, model training, and feedback loops are essential to building a system that serves users from all backgrounds equitably.

By recognizing that bias and fairness are ongoing challenges rather than fixed problems, GPT-5 can be developed and used in ways that minimize harm while maximizing its value as a truly global conversational partner.

Responsible Use Guidelines

The power and versatility of ChatGPT-5 bring with them an obligation to use the system in a way that benefits individuals and society while avoiding harm. Responsible use is about ensuring that interactions with the model are safe, ethical, and constructive. These guidelines provide a framework for achieving that goal.

1. Verify Important Information
Although GPT-5 is capable of generating detailed and convincing responses, it is not infallible. Always verify critical facts with reliable and up-to-date sources, especially in fields such as medicine, law, finance, or science. Treat GPT-5 as an assistant for idea generation and analysis, not as an unquestionable authority.

2. Avoid Harmful or Unsafe Content
Do not use GPT-5 to create, promote, or distribute content that could cause harm. This includes violence, self-harm, harassment, illegal activities, or misinformation. If the model produces an unsafe or inappropriate response, stop and reframe the request or seek an alternative approach.

3. Respect Privacy and Confidentiality
Never provide GPT-5 with sensitive personal information, whether your own or someone else's. Avoid inputting confidential corporate data or private communications unless the system is being used in a secure, authorized environment.

4. Be Aware of Bias
GPT-5 can reflect biases present in its training data. When dealing with topics involving culture, identity, or ethics, review the model's outputs for fairness and balance. Seek diverse perspectives and avoid

relying on a single AI-generated answer when the issue is sensitive or complex.

5. Use the Model Within Legal and Ethical Boundaries
Follow all applicable laws and ethical standards in your location and field of work. For example, do not use GPT-5 to impersonate individuals, violate copyright protections, or engage in fraudulent activities.

6. Apply Transparency in AI-Assisted Work
If GPT-5 significantly contributes to a piece of writing, analysis, or creative work, consider disclosing that AI assistance was used. Transparency builds trust with audiences and allows others to interpret the content in context.

7. Use Contextual Framing in Prompts
To improve both accuracy and ethical reliability, provide GPT-5 with clear context for your requests. Ambiguous or poorly structured prompts increase the risk of inaccurate or misleading outputs.

8. Promote Constructive Use
Harness GPT-5 for purposes that add value, such as education, problem-solving, research, creativity, and accessibility. Avoid using the technology in ways that exploit individuals or communities.

Why Responsible Use Matters
AI models like GPT-5 can amplify both good and bad outcomes depending on how they are used. Responsible use ensures that the benefits - such as enhanced productivity, greater access to knowledge, and creative collaboration - are achieved without creating unnecessary risks or harm.

By following responsible use guidelines, individuals and organizations can maximize the value of GPT-5 while supporting ethical, safe, and beneficial interactions. The goal is not just to use the tool effectively, but to ensure its contributions are aligned with the principles of respect, fairness, and societal good.

OpenAI's Safeguards and Moderation

OpenAI has implemented a multi-layered system of safeguards and moderation tools in ChatGPT-5 to reduce the risks associated with harmful, unsafe, or unethical outputs. These safeguards work in combination with technical design choices, human oversight, and user reporting systems to promote safe and responsible use of the model.

1. Content Filtering Systems

Before a response is shown to the user, GPT-5's outputs are evaluated against a set of content guidelines. These guidelines are designed to block or modify responses that involve explicit violence, hate speech, harassment, sexual content involving minors, promotion of self-harm, or illegal activities. The filtering system operates in real time to prevent most unsafe content from reaching the user.

2. Prompt Analysis

Safeguards begin before the model generates text. The system analyzes user prompts to identify requests that may lead to unsafe or prohibited content. If such prompts are detected, GPT-5 may refuse to answer, provide a safe rephrasing, or guide the user toward a more appropriate request.

3. Fine-Tuning for Safety

Part of GPT-5's training involves fine-tuning on curated datasets that emphasize safe and ethical responses. This includes examples where unsafe or biased outputs are replaced with neutral, constructive alternatives. Reinforcement learning from human feedback (RLHF) is also applied to teach the model how to handle sensitive topics while still being helpful.

4. Layered Moderation Models

OpenAI uses dedicated moderation models that run alongside GPT-5 to classify inputs and outputs according to safety categories. These models act as a checkpoint, ensuring that potentially harmful content is flagged, blocked, or redirected for review.

5. User Feedback Loops

Users can report problematic responses directly through the ChatGPT interface. These reports are reviewed by human moderators, and if patterns of unsafe behavior are identified, they inform updates to the filtering and moderation systems. This feedback process helps refine safety measures over time.

6. Adaptive Risk Controls

OpenAI continuously updates safeguards to respond to emerging risks. For example, if a new type of misuse is identified, rules and filters can be updated to prevent it in future interactions. This ensures that GPT-5's safety mechanisms evolve alongside changes in user behavior and societal context.

7. Transparency in Limitations

When GPT-5 declines to answer or modifies a response for safety reasons, it often communicates that decision to the user. This transparency helps build understanding of the boundaries set by the moderation system and reinforces the principle that safety takes priority over unrestricted output.

The Role of Safeguards in Responsible AI

Safeguards and moderation do not eliminate all risks, but they significantly reduce the likelihood of harmful interactions. They also encourage trust between users and the system by showing that OpenAI is actively managing the ethical implications of its technology. By combining automated filtering, human oversight, and community feedback, GPT-5's safety framework supports a balance between open expression and responsible use.

Part II: Practical Usage and Techniques

Chapter 5 – Getting Started with ChatGPT-5

Setting Up Accounts and Interfaces

Getting started with ChatGPT-5 begins with creating an account and learning how to navigate its available interfaces. Whether you are accessing the model through OpenAI's official platform or via an integrated third-party service, the process is straightforward once you understand the basic steps.

1. Creating an OpenAI Account
To use ChatGPT-5 directly from OpenAI, you need an OpenAI account. The setup process usually involves:

- Visiting the official OpenAI website.
- Selecting the "Sign Up" option.
- Providing an email address, creating a password, or using a supported single sign-on option such as Google or Microsoft login.
- Verifying your email address through a confirmation link.
- Providing a phone number for identity verification, which helps reduce misuse of the service.

Once the account is created and verified, you can access ChatGPT-5 through the web interface, desktop application, or mobile app, depending on availability.

2. Subscription Plans
OpenAI typically offers both free and paid subscription options. The free plan allows access to a basic version of ChatGPT with some limitations in speed, availability, or feature access. The paid subscription, often branded as ChatGPT Plus or similar, grants

priority access, faster responses, and access to the latest model version such as GPT-5. Selecting a plan depends on your intended use, budget, and need for advanced features.

3. Choosing Your Access Method
ChatGPT-5 can be used through several types of interfaces:

- **Web Interface**: Accessible through a browser at the official OpenAI site, offering a simple text-based chat window and settings menu.
- **Mobile App**: Available for iOS and Android, enabling quick access and portability.
- **Desktop App**: In some cases, downloadable software for Windows or macOS provides a dedicated environment for extended use.
- **API Access**: For developers and organizations, the OpenAI API allows integration of GPT-5 into custom applications, websites, and workflows.

4. Configuring Your Workspace
After logging in, you can configure preferences such as conversation history, interface theme (light or dark mode), and default model version. For professional or collaborative environments, you may also set up shared workspaces where team members can access and use the model with shared settings.

5. Understanding the Interface
Most ChatGPT-5 interfaces include:

- A **prompt input field** where you type your requests or questions.
- A **response area** where the model's replies appear.
- A **settings menu** where you can select the model version, manage your account, or adjust conversation preferences.

- An **export or copy feature** to save outputs for later use.
- A **feedback tool** for reporting problematic outputs or rating responses.

6. Securing Your Account
Enable two-factor authentication (2FA) if available to protect your account. Avoid sharing login credentials, especially if you use the account for sensitive or professional purposes. If using API keys, store them securely and restrict access to authorized users only.

7. First Steps After Setup
Once the account and interface are ready, start with small test prompts to become familiar with how GPT-5 responds. Experiment with different types of requests - such as creative writing, research summaries, or code generation - to understand its strengths and limits.

By setting up your account correctly and learning the available interfaces, you establish a solid foundation for using ChatGPT-5 effectively. This preparation ensures you can focus on exploring its capabilities without technical obstacles getting in the way.

Free vs. Paid Versions

When you begin using ChatGPT-5, one of the first decisions to make is whether to use the free version or subscribe to the paid plan. Both options give you access to the core experience of interacting with the model, but there are important differences in performance, availability, and feature access that can influence your choice.

1. Free Version
The free version is designed to provide basic access to ChatGPT for casual or light users. It typically includes:

- Access to a previous or limited model version rather than the most advanced release.

- Slower response times during high demand periods since paying subscribers receive priority.
- A limited number of messages or tokens per set time period.
- Fewer customization and advanced setting options.
- Occasional downtime during peak hours when server capacity is fully used.

The free version is ideal for users who want to explore ChatGPT-5's general capabilities, experiment with prompts, or use it for non-time-sensitive tasks. It is also useful for learning the basics before deciding whether the paid features are worth the investment.

2. Paid Version (ChatGPT Plus or Equivalent)
The paid plan, often referred to as ChatGPT Plus or a similar tier, unlocks the full potential of GPT-5. It usually includes:

- Guaranteed access to the latest and most capable model version, such as GPT-5, instead of an earlier release.
- Priority access during busy times, which means faster responses and less downtime.
- Higher usage limits for both message count and token capacity.
- Early access to new features and experimental tools.
- Improved performance for demanding tasks such as extended research, code generation, or high-volume content creation.

The paid version is well-suited for professionals, educators, content creators, researchers, and developers who depend on consistent performance and advanced capabilities. The speed and availability advantages alone can make it valuable for business-critical or time-sensitive work.

3. Deciding Which Option to Choose

Your choice between the free and paid versions depends on your usage pattern:

- Choose the **free version** if your needs are casual, you are exploring the tool for the first time, or you only require occasional access.
- Choose the **paid version** if you need consistent access, faster speeds, and the latest capabilities, or if you plan to use GPT-5 for professional or high-stakes applications.

4. Transitioning from Free to Paid

You can start with the free version and upgrade to the paid plan at any time. This allows you to test GPT-5's general functionality before committing. Once upgraded, you can immediately take advantage of the latest model, faster performance, and increased limits without losing your existing account history or saved settings.

Understanding the trade-offs between free and paid versions ensures that you select the plan that best matches your goals. By making an informed decision, you can maximize the value you get from ChatGPT-5 while avoiding unnecessary costs.

Here's a clear comparison table showing the main differences between the free and paid versions of ChatGPT-5.

Feature	**Free Version**	**Paid Version (ChatGPT Plus or Equivalent)**
Model Access	Limited or earlier version of GPT (not always GPT-5)	Latest and most capable model (GPT-5)

Feature	Free Version	Paid Version (ChatGPT Plus or Equivalent)
Response Speed	Standard speed, may slow during peak hours	Faster response times, even during high demand
Availability	Lower priority; possible downtime in busy periods	Priority access; minimal or no downtime
Usage Limits	Limited number of messages or tokens per time period	Higher limits for messages and tokens
Feature Access	Basic features only	Early access to new tools and experimental features
Customization Options	Limited control over style and tone	Greater customization and advanced settings
Best For	Casual use, experimentation, learning basics	Professional, academic, and high-demand tasks

Navigating Settings and Features

Once your ChatGPT-5 account is set up, knowing how to navigate its settings and features is essential for getting the best experience. The interface is designed to be user-friendly, but understanding where key tools are located and how to adjust them can greatly improve productivity and personalization.

1. Accessing the Settings Menu
In most versions of ChatGPT-5, the settings icon is located in a sidebar or in the upper corner of the interface. Clicking it will open a panel or menu that allows you to configure account preferences, adjust conversation settings, and manage interface options.

2. Choosing the Model Version
If you have access to multiple model versions, the settings menu typically allows you to choose which one to use. Free accounts may be limited to a smaller or earlier model, while paid accounts can select GPT-5 for maximum capability. Choosing the right model can impact both response quality and speed.

3. Adjusting Conversation History
Users can toggle whether ChatGPT-5 remembers past conversations in the current session or across sessions. Disabling conversation history can improve privacy but means the model will not retain earlier context once the chat is closed. Enabling it allows smoother continuity for ongoing projects.

4. Theme and Display Preferences
Many interfaces allow switching between light and dark modes, adjusting font size, or modifying message spacing. These visual settings do not affect the model's performance but can improve comfort during long sessions.

5. Configuring Output Style and Tone
Some settings allow users to choose default tones (such as formal, casual, or instructional) or control the level of detail in responses. While you can set tone in individual prompts, having a default style can save time for repeated tasks.

6. Managing API Keys
For developers integrating GPT-5 into their own applications, the settings menu often includes a section for generating and managing

API keys. These should be stored securely and never shared publicly, as they grant direct access to the model's capabilities.

7. Using Additional Features
Depending on the platform, ChatGPT-5 may include extra tools such as:

- **File Uploads**: Allowing the model to analyze documents, spreadsheets, or images.
- **Multimodal Inputs**: Enabling both text and image queries in the same session.
- **Voice Input and Output**: Letting you speak to the model and receive audio responses.
- **Prompt Templates**: Pre-made instructions for common tasks like summarization, translation, or brainstorming.

8. Safety and Moderation Controls
In some implementations, users can adjust sensitivity levels for content moderation. This can help tailor responses for specific audiences, such as educational environments.

9. Exporting and Saving Responses
The settings menu often includes options for downloading conversation transcripts, copying text, or exporting data in formats like PDF or plain text. This is useful for record-keeping or integrating GPT-5's outputs into other workflows.

10. Feedback and Reporting
Users can report problematic responses directly through the interface. This feedback is reviewed by OpenAI to help refine model safety and performance.

Why Navigating Settings Matters
Taking time to explore the settings ensures that you can customize ChatGPT-5 to fit your needs, work more efficiently, and maintain

control over privacy and safety. It transforms the model from a general-purpose assistant into a tailored tool that matches your personal or professional requirements.

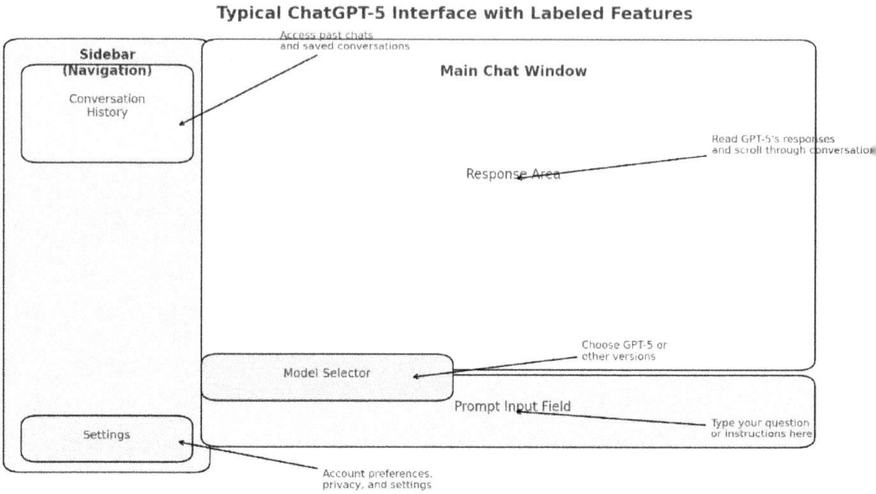

Chapter 6 – Prompt Engineering Basics

What Prompts Are and Why They Matter

A prompt is the instruction, question, or statement you give to ChatGPT-5 to guide its response. It is the starting point for every interaction and determines the direction, clarity, and usefulness of the output. While prompts may seem as simple as typing a question, their structure and wording have a major impact on the quality of results you receive.

1. Definition of a Prompt

In the context of ChatGPT-5, a prompt is the text you provide as input. It can range from a single word to multiple paragraphs of detailed instructions. The model uses the prompt to determine what information is relevant, what tone to adopt, and how to format its response.

2. How Prompts Influence Output

The way you phrase your prompt affects the depth, accuracy, and creativity of the model's reply. For example:

- **Vague prompt**: "Tell me about space" may result in a broad, generic answer.
- **Specific prompt**: "Explain the process of star formation in simple terms for a high school science project" will likely produce a more targeted and relevant response.

The more specific and clear your prompt, the better the model can meet your expectations.

3. Why Prompts Matter

Prompts matter because they:

- **Define the context**: Without clear context, the model may guess your intent incorrectly.

- **Control the style and tone**: You can ask for formal, casual, humorous, or technical responses simply by stating it in the prompt.
- **Determine the level of detail**: Adding constraints such as "in 200 words" or "include bullet points" guides the model's format.
- **Shape creativity**: A creative or open-ended prompt can lead to unique and innovative outputs.

4. Prompts as a Skill

Prompt writing is not only about asking a question but about framing it in a way that maximizes the model's ability to help you. This is why prompt engineering is considered a skill in its own right. Over time, you can learn patterns, structures, and strategies that consistently produce higher-quality outputs.

5. Examples of Effective Prompting

- **Instruction-based**: "Write a 150-word summary of the key differences between GPT-4 and GPT-5."
- **Role-based**: "You are an expert travel planner. Create a 5-day itinerary for Tokyo focused on cultural attractions."
- **Step-by-step requests**: "Explain the water cycle in three stages, with each stage in one sentence."

By understanding what prompts are and why they matter, you gain the foundation for crafting better instructions, which leads to more accurate, useful, and creative responses from ChatGPT-5. The prompt is the steering wheel for your interaction, and learning how to use it well is key to mastering the model.

Crafting Clear and Concise Prompts

The quality of ChatGPT-5's responses depends heavily on how clearly and precisely you frame your prompt. While the model is capable of interpreting a wide range of inputs, ambiguous or poorly structured prompts often lead to incomplete or unfocused answers. Crafting a clear and concise prompt ensures the model understands exactly what you want and can deliver the most relevant output.

1. Be Specific About Your Goal

A good prompt communicates your intent without leaving too much room for misinterpretation. Instead of saying "Tell me about history," specify the period, event, or perspective you want. For example:

- Vague: "Tell me about history."
- Clear: "Explain the causes and consequences of the French Revolution in under 300 words."

2. Include Relevant Context

Adding background information helps the model tailor its response to your needs. For instance:

- Instead of: "Write about climate change."
- Use: "Write a 200-word summary on climate change suitable for a 10th-grade science class, focusing on its main causes and effects."

3. Define the Output Format

Tell the model how you want the answer structured. You can ask for bullet points, numbered lists, short paragraphs, or a specific style. Examples:

- "List five bullet points summarizing the benefits of solar power."
- "Create a formal letter of recommendation for a software engineer."

4. Limit Ambiguity

Avoid vague terms unless you want open-ended creativity. Words like "good," "interesting," or "about" can mean different things in different contexts. Instead, use precise descriptors like "three main economic advantages" or "step-by-step tutorial."

5. Keep It Concise but Complete
Your prompt should be detailed enough to guide the model, yet short enough to read and understand at a glance. Long, overly complex prompts can confuse the model, while short, unclear prompts can result in generic answers. A balanced prompt gives the model all necessary instructions without unnecessary filler.

6. Use Examples When Needed
If you want the model to mimic a certain style or tone, provide an example. For example:

- "Write a poem about the moon in the style of this short example: [Insert poem]."

7. Test and Refine Your Prompts
Prompt engineering is an iterative process. If the output is not what you expect, rephrase your prompt with clearer wording, additional context, or explicit instructions on format. Over time, you will learn which phrasing patterns produce the best results for your specific needs.

8. Practice Role Assignments
Assigning the model a role can lead to more accurate and tailored responses. For example:

- "You are a legal consultant. Draft a one-page summary of the new privacy regulation for small businesses."

Why Clear and Concise Prompts Matter
A well-crafted prompt acts as a precise roadmap for the model. It minimizes confusion, saves time by reducing the need for repeated clarifications, and maximizes the relevance and quality of the

response. The clearer your instructions, the more likely ChatGPT-5 will deliver exactly what you are looking for.

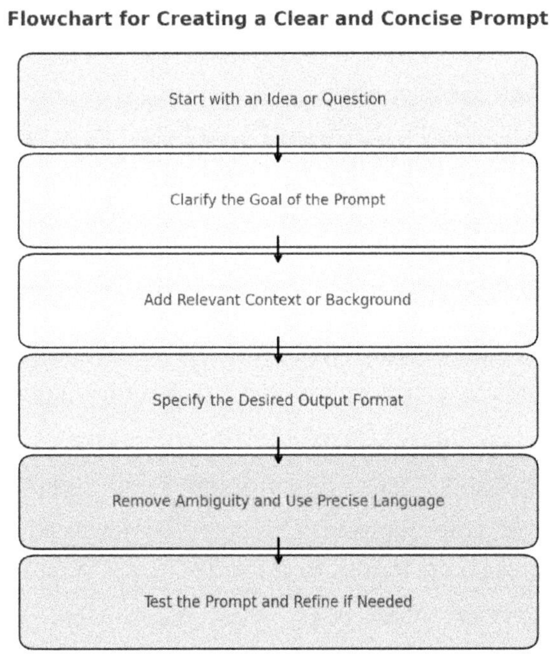

Role Assignment and Context Setting

Role assignment and context setting are two of the most powerful techniques in prompt engineering. They allow you to frame your request in a way that guides ChatGPT-5 toward producing responses that match a specific perspective, tone, and expertise level. By assigning a role, you effectively tell the model to "think like" a particular type of person or entity. By providing context, you supply the background information needed for the model to generate accurate and relevant content.

1. What is Role Assignment?

Role assignment is when you instruct ChatGPT-5 to act as a specific persona or professional. This can range from creative roles, such as

"You are a poet writing in the style of William Wordsworth," to professional ones like "You are a data scientist explaining statistical models to business executives." The role sets the tone, vocabulary, and knowledge depth of the response.

Benefits of Role Assignment:

- **Tailored expertise**: You receive information framed through the lens of a particular skill set or profession.
- **Consistent tone**: Responses maintain a style that matches your desired audience.
- **Creative direction**: The model can mimic historical figures, fictional characters, or industry experts for unique results.

2. What is Context Setting?

Context setting involves giving the model background information before it answers your question. This could be details about your audience, purpose, constraints, or prior discussion points. For example:

- Without context: "Explain photosynthesis."
- With context: "Explain photosynthesis in simple language for a group of 8-year-old students who have just learned about plant parts."

By including relevant context, you increase the likelihood that the response will be accurate, focused, and fit for your intended purpose.

3. Combining Role and Context

The most effective prompts often combine both techniques. For example:

- "You are a friendly science teacher preparing a 5-minute classroom talk. Explain the process of earthquakes using simple terms and include one analogy to everyday life."

This prompt tells the model who it is pretending to be, who the audience is, how long the explanation should be, and even what style of example to include.

4. Best Practices for Role Assignment and Context Setting

- **Be explicit**: State the role clearly, such as "act as," "you are," or "pretend you are."
- **Match role to audience**: Ensure the chosen role fits the needs of your readers or listeners.
- **Provide all relevant details**: Include information about tone, format, length, or any constraints.
- **Avoid overloading**: While context is important, too much unnecessary detail can distract from the main task.

5. Examples of Role and Context Use

- **Professional**: "You are an HR consultant. Write a job description for a junior software developer in a small startup."
- **Creative**: "You are a mystery novelist. Write the first paragraph of a suspenseful story set in 19th-century London."
- **Instructional**: "You are a language tutor. Explain the difference between 'since' and 'for' in English grammar to a beginner-level student."

Why This Matters

When ChatGPT-5 knows "who" it is supposed to be and understands the situation in which it is speaking, its responses are significantly more aligned with your goals. This combination improves clarity, ensures relevance, and enhances the overall usefulness of the model's output.

Relationship Between Role Assignment, Context Setting, and Output Quality

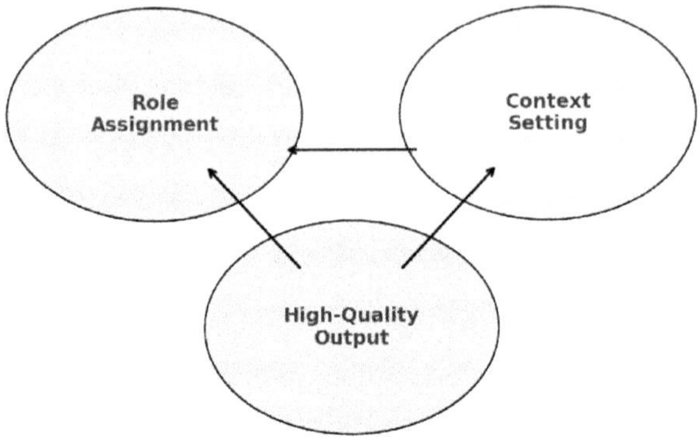

Chapter 7 – Advanced Prompting Strategies

Chain-of-Thought Prompting

Chain-of-thought prompting is an advanced prompting strategy designed to guide ChatGPT-5 through a step-by-step reasoning process rather than asking it to jump directly to the final answer. This approach encourages the model to break down complex problems into smaller, logical steps, which often leads to more accurate and transparent results.

1. What is Chain-of-Thought Prompting?

Chain-of-thought prompting involves explicitly telling the model to think through a problem before answering. Instead of producing an immediate conclusion, the model is encouraged to outline the reasoning path that leads to the answer. This is particularly valuable for tasks that require analysis, problem-solving, or logical deduction.

2. Why It Works

Large language models like ChatGPT-5 excel at pattern recognition and contextual reasoning. By prompting them to explain their thought process, you activate these reasoning pathways in a structured manner. This approach reduces the likelihood of skipping steps or making unsupported assumptions.

3. When to Use It

This technique is most effective for:

- **Mathematical problems**: "Solve this equation step by step: $2x + 5 = 15$."
- **Logical puzzles**: "Explain your reasoning in finding the murderer in this mystery."
- **Complex decision-making**: "List the factors to consider when choosing between two business strategies and explain how each factor affects the decision."

- **Data interpretation**: "Describe how you reached your conclusion when analyzing these statistics."

4. How to Apply Chain-of-Thought Prompting

- **Be explicit in your request**: Use phrases like "Explain your reasoning," "Walk me through the steps," or "Show your thought process before giving the answer."
- **Break the task into sub-tasks**: You can manually guide the model by asking one sub-question at a time, leading to the final conclusion.
- **Encourage detail**: Ask for enough detail so that each step logically follows from the previous one.

5. Example

Instead of:

"What is 25% of 360?"
You might write:
"Explain step by step how to calculate 25% of 360 and then provide the final answer."

This ensures that the model first explains how percentages work, then performs the multiplication, and finally delivers the answer.

6. Advantages of Chain-of-Thought Prompting

- Improves accuracy for multi-step problems.
- Makes the reasoning process visible, which helps in identifying and correcting errors.
- Enhances learning by allowing users to follow the logic behind the answer.
- Builds trust in the output since the reasoning is transparent.

7. Limitations

- Longer responses may be generated, which can be less efficient for very simple queries.
- The model's reasoning is not truly human thought, so while it can appear logical, it may occasionally contain flawed or irrelevant steps.

Why This Matters

Chain-of-thought prompting transforms ChatGPT-5 from a tool that simply provides answers into a reasoning partner that reveals its process. For professionals, educators, and learners, this is invaluable for ensuring accuracy, transparency, and a deeper understanding of the solution.

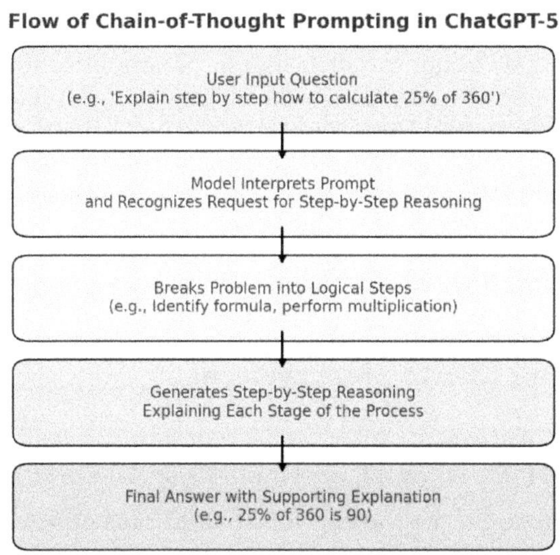

Multi-turn Conversation Management

Multi-turn conversation management refers to the techniques used to maintain coherent and productive dialogues with ChatGPT-5 over multiple exchanges. While single-turn prompts involve asking a question and getting one response, multi-turn conversations are more dynamic and resemble a true back-and-forth discussion. They allow you to refine outputs, build on previous answers, and work toward complex goals over several interactions.

1. Understanding Multi-turn Conversations

In a multi-turn setting, the model keeps track of prior messages in the conversation. This enables it to reference past information, maintain consistency in tone or role, and address follow-up questions. For example, if you ask, "Explain the causes of the French Revolution," and then follow with "Now summarize that in three bullet points," the model will understand "that" refers to the causes it just explained.

2. Benefits of Multi-turn Conversation Management

- **Improved depth and clarity**: You can progressively refine outputs by asking for elaboration or simplification.
- **Consistency in tone and perspective**: The model remembers your role assignments or stylistic choices across turns.
- **Efficient problem-solving**: You can work through multi-step projects without repeating all the details in each prompt.

3. Strategies for Effective Management

a. Maintain Context

Although ChatGPT-5 has a large context window, you should restate critical information if it is central to the task. This ensures the model stays aligned, especially in long conversations.

b. Use Incremental Refinement

Start with a broad request, then narrow down the details in subsequent turns. For example:

1. "Give me an overview of renewable energy sources."

2. "Focus on solar energy and explain its advantages and disadvantages."
3. "Now provide three real-world examples of solar projects in Asia."

c. Reference Previous Responses Explicitly
If you want the model to adjust or expand an earlier answer, refer to it directly: "In your earlier explanation about solar energy, add more technical details about photovoltaic cells."

d. Keep Objectives Clear
Even though the model remembers prior turns, clearly stating your goal in each follow-up helps avoid misunderstandings.

4. Potential Challenges

- **Context overflow**: In very long conversations, older parts of the discussion may fall outside the context window and be forgotten.
- **Unintended shifts in tone**: Without reminders, the model may drift away from the desired style.
- **Loss of focus**: Conversations can wander if prompts are not kept on track.

5. Best Practices

- Periodically summarize the key points covered so far.
- Reiterate constraints or requirements in longer threads.
- Use turn-based refinements to build toward the final result.
- Save important outputs externally so they can be reintroduced if context is lost.

Why This Matters
Effective multi-turn conversation management transforms ChatGPT-

5 from a question-answer tool into a collaborative partner. It allows you to handle complex projects, research tasks, and creative processes with continuity and precision, while also maximizing the efficiency of your interactions.

Multi-Turn Conversation Flow in ChatGPT-5

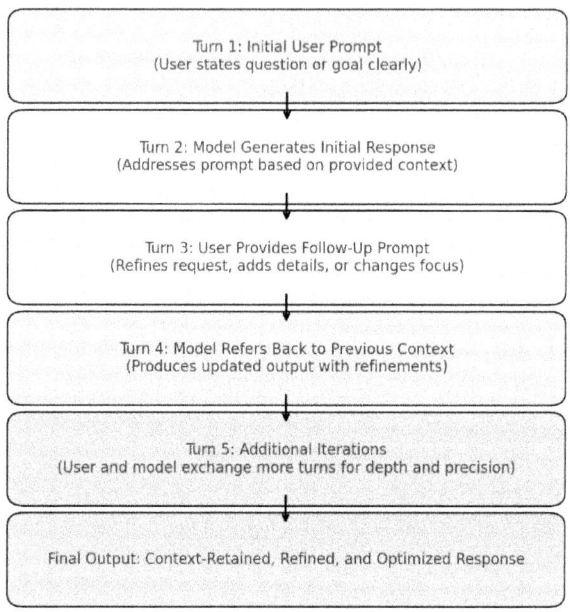

Creative, Analytical, and Hybrid Prompts

Prompts can be designed to achieve different types of outputs depending on your objectives. Some prompts aim to inspire original, imaginative ideas, while others focus on precise reasoning and factual accuracy. A hybrid prompt combines elements of both, guiding ChatGPT-5 to produce results that are both innovative and logically sound. Understanding these categories allows you to select the right approach for your needs.

1. Creative Prompts
Creative prompts are designed to encourage originality, imagination, and expressive output. They often leave room for interpretation and invite the model to explore possibilities without strict constraints.

- **Purpose**: To generate stories, poetry, ideas, or concepts that go beyond factual explanation.
- **Best Use Cases**: Creative writing, brainstorming, marketing copy, fictional scenarios, or artistic projects.
- **Example**: "Write a short science fiction story about a city that floats above the clouds, narrated by a robot."

Tips for Creative Prompts:

- Use open-ended questions or scenarios.
- Encourage vivid descriptions and sensory detail.
- Avoid over-restricting the scope, allowing room for exploration.

2. Analytical Prompts
Analytical prompts require careful reasoning, logical thinking, and structured explanations. They focus on producing factual, evidence-based responses rather than open-ended imagination.

- **Purpose**: To explain concepts, solve problems, interpret data, or provide critical analysis.
- **Best Use Cases**: Academic research, technical writing, data analysis, or professional advice.
- **Example**: "Analyze the potential economic impacts of renewable energy adoption in developing countries, including both benefits and challenges."

Tips for Analytical Prompts:

- Be specific about the scope and depth of analysis required.
- Provide relevant background information to guide reasoning.
- Define the expected structure, such as bullet points, reports, or step-by-step explanations.

3. Hybrid Prompts

Hybrid prompts combine creative thinking with analytical precision. They are valuable when you need solutions that are both imaginative and grounded in logic.

- **Purpose**: To generate innovative yet realistic outputs that balance originality with sound reasoning.
- **Best Use Cases**: Strategic planning, product design, content creation with factual grounding, or scenario-based problem-solving.
- **Example**: "As an urban planner, design a futuristic city powered entirely by renewable energy. Include imaginative architectural features and provide a feasibility analysis for the proposed technology."

Tips for Hybrid Prompts:

- Clearly outline both creative and analytical requirements.
- Balance open-ended exploration with specific factual elements.
- Indicate whether the response should separate the creative and analytical sections or blend them together.

Why This Matters

Knowing when to use creative, analytical, or hybrid prompts allows you to maximize ChatGPT-5's capabilities. Creative prompts help unlock innovation, analytical prompts ensure precision and factual reliability, and hybrid prompts give you the best of both worlds. By matching the prompt type to your goal, you can guide the model toward producing results that are relevant, effective, and engaging.

Chapter 8 – Multimodal Interaction

Using Text Plus Images

One of the most powerful features of ChatGPT-5 is its ability to handle multimodal inputs. This means the model can process both text and images together to produce a more context-aware and relevant response. Using text plus images allows users to communicate ideas, questions, and instructions in richer and more efficient ways.

1. What It Means to Combine Text and Images

When you provide both text and an image, ChatGPT-5 processes them as related inputs. The text supplies context, instructions, or questions, while the image provides visual data. The model merges these inputs to deliver answers that take both sources of information into account. For example, you could upload a chart and ask the model to summarize trends shown in it.

2. Benefits of Text Plus Image Interaction

- **Enhanced clarity**: Visual content can reduce ambiguity in text descriptions.
- **Better understanding of complex subjects**: Images help illustrate details that would take many words to describe.
- **Faster problem-solving**: By pairing a visual reference with a targeted question, you can get more precise answers quickly.
- **Supports creativity**: The model can generate captions, visual analyses, or creative stories inspired by images.

3. How to Use This Feature Effectively

- **Always provide clear context**: Even if the image is self-explanatory, a short text description helps the model interpret it correctly.

- **Ask specific questions**: Instead of saying "Describe this image," you could say "Explain what the graph shows about rainfall patterns over the last decade."
- **Use text to guide the purpose**: Specify whether you want an analysis, a creative interpretation, or factual identification.
- **Check visual interpretation carefully**: The model's understanding of images may depend on clarity, resolution, and relevance.

4. Example Scenarios

- **Educational use**: A teacher uploads a diagram of the human heart and asks for an age-appropriate explanation for middle school students.
- **Business reports**: An analyst uploads a financial chart and requests a summary of quarterly performance trends.
- **Creative work**: A writer uploads a photograph of a sunset and asks for a poem inspired by its colors and mood.
- **Technical troubleshooting**: An engineer uploads a machine part photo and asks for possible reasons it might malfunction.

5. Best Practices

- Ensure your images are clear and relevant to your query.
- Pair visual content with enough textual detail to remove guesswork.
- If multiple images are used, reference them by name or order in your text prompt.
- Review results to confirm the interpretation aligns with your goals.

Why This Matters

Text plus image interaction expands ChatGPT-5's capabilities beyond simple written responses. It allows users to communicate in ways that better reflect real-world problem-solving, where information is rarely only verbal or only visual. This fusion of modalities enables richer, more accurate, and more engaging AI conversations.

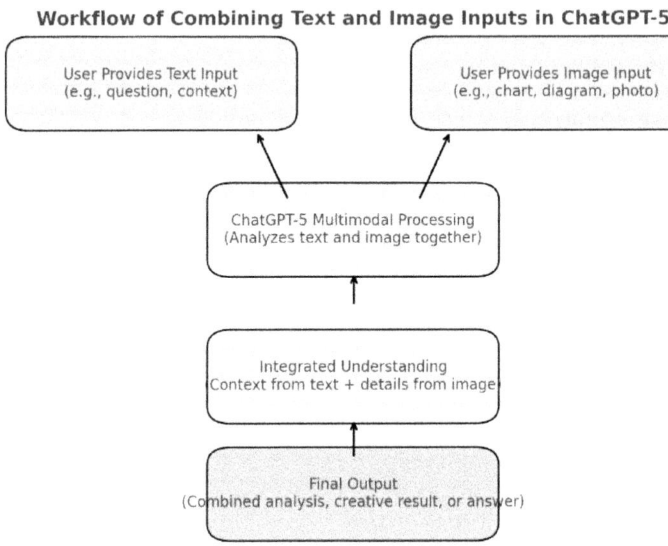

Audio-Based Input and Output

ChatGPT-5 has advanced capabilities for understanding and generating audio, making it a versatile tool for tasks that go beyond written communication. By integrating speech-to-text and text-to-speech technologies, the model can accept spoken queries, process them with the same language understanding as text inputs, and deliver responses in audio form. This creates a more natural, hands-free, and accessible way to interact with AI.

1. How Audio Input Works

Audio input relies on speech recognition systems that convert spoken words into text. Once the audio is transcribed, ChatGPT-5 processes it just as it would process typed input. This allows for conversational interactions without the need for a keyboard.

- **Example**: A user says, "Summarize today's top news headlines," and the system converts the speech into text before passing it to the model for processing.

2. How Audio Output Works
For audio output, ChatGPT-5 uses text-to-speech technology to turn its written responses into spoken language. The tone, pitch, and pacing can often be adjusted for clarity or personalization.

- **Example**: Instead of reading a recipe on-screen, the model can read it aloud step by step so the user can follow along while cooking.

3. Benefits of Audio-Based Interaction

- **Accessibility**: Helps users with visual impairments or reading difficulties interact with the model more easily.
- **Convenience**: Enables hands-free operation for multitasking or on-the-go use.
- **Engagement**: Provides a more conversational and human-like experience.
- **Language Learning**: Supports pronunciation practice and listening comprehension.

4. Use Cases

- **Education**: Teachers can speak questions and have the model read back explanations for students.
- **Customer Service**: Businesses can integrate audio-based ChatGPT-5 interactions into phone support systems.

- **Personal Assistance**: Users can ask for reminders, schedules, or quick facts while driving or cooking.
- **Entertainment**: The model can narrate stories or create interactive audio-based games.

5. Best Practices

- Speak clearly and avoid background noise for better transcription accuracy.
- For complex tasks, provide key details in a single spoken prompt to reduce misunderstanding.
- When using audio output, adjust the voice settings to match the use case, whether that is formal, casual, fast-paced, or slow and clear.
- Review the transcription of your spoken input to confirm it matches your intent before the model responds.

Why This Matters
Audio-based interaction with ChatGPT-5 makes AI communication more inclusive, flexible, and human-centered. It allows people to use natural speech patterns and receive information in ways that best suit their needs and environments, expanding the accessibility and usability of AI in everyday life.

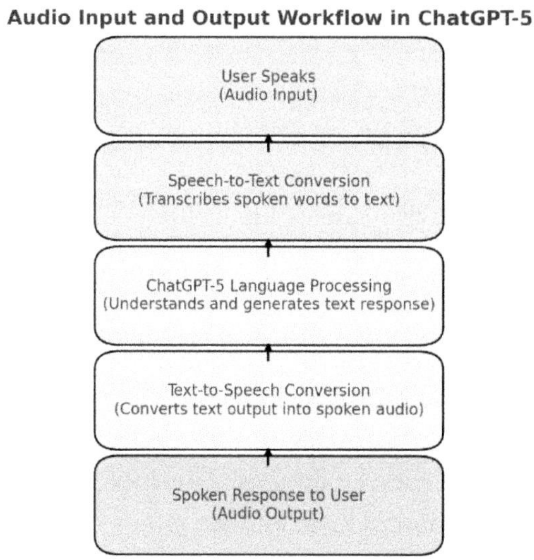

Visual Analysis and Creative Generation

ChatGPT-5 is capable of more than simply describing images. It can analyze visual content for patterns, extract detailed information, and even generate creative ideas based on what it sees. This ability makes it a valuable tool for education, design, research, and entertainment. By combining strong image interpretation with creative thinking, the model can address both analytical and imaginative needs.

1. Visual Analysis

Visual analysis involves examining images to identify objects, relationships, and patterns. The model can interpret diagrams, charts, technical schematics, photographs, and artistic works.

- **Example for data interpretation**: An uploaded sales chart can be analyzed for trends, seasonal patterns, and anomalies.
- **Example for object recognition**: A picture of a street can be broken down into identifiable elements such as vehicles, buildings, and pedestrians.

- **Example for contextual understanding**: A photo of a plant can be used to identify its species and suggest care instructions.

Key strengths in analysis:

- Recognizing objects, text, and symbols in images.
- Explaining relationships between elements.
- Summarizing complex visuals into concise explanations.

2. Creative Generation from Visuals
In creative generation, the model uses the image as inspiration to produce new ideas, stories, or designs. This is particularly useful in fields like marketing, storytelling, and art.

- **Example for storytelling**: A photograph of an abandoned house can inspire a suspenseful short story.
- **Example for design ideas**: A picture of a kitchen can be the starting point for proposing renovation styles.
- **Example for concept art**: An abstract painting can inspire the description of a fantasy world.

Tips for effective creative generation:

- Give clear instructions on tone, style, or purpose.
- Combine the visual with a guiding question or theme.
- Provide boundaries if you want the creativity to remain realistic.

3. Combining Analysis and Creativity
Some use cases require both analytical and creative elements. For instance, a company may upload a product photo for analysis of its current design and request creative suggestions for improvement.

This approach ensures that the output is grounded in accurate visual interpretation while also exploring innovative possibilities.

4. Best Practices

- Use high-quality and clear images for better accuracy.
- Include any necessary background context to guide interpretation.
- Specify whether the focus should be on factual accuracy, creativity, or both.
- Review outputs for accuracy, especially in professional or technical contexts.

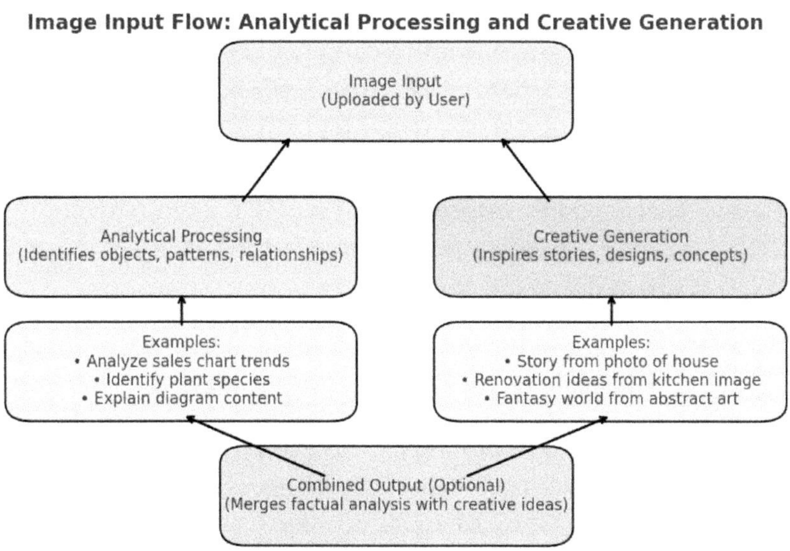

Chapter 9 – Automation and Integration

Connecting ChatGPT-5 to APIs

Connecting ChatGPT-5 to external Application Programming Interfaces (APIs) allows it to become a dynamic, interactive tool capable of pulling in real-time data, performing transactions, and interacting with other software systems. This integration transforms ChatGPT-5 from a conversational model into a functional component within larger automated workflows.

1. What It Means to Connect ChatGPT-5 to an API

An API acts as a bridge between ChatGPT-5 and another system. Through this bridge, ChatGPT-5 can send requests and receive responses in structured formats such as JSON. The model can use this information to provide up-to-date answers, control external systems, or perform specific tasks based on real-world data.

2. Benefits of API Integration

- **Access to live information**: ChatGPT-5 can retrieve weather forecasts, stock prices, news headlines, or other current data.
- **Automation**: It can trigger workflows like sending emails, scheduling appointments, or updating databases.
- **Extended functionality**: APIs can allow ChatGPT-5 to handle specialized tasks such as language translation, payment processing, or social media posting.
- **Personalization**: Integration with user data APIs enables responses tailored to specific needs or preferences.

3. How API Integration Works

1. **Identify the API**: Choose the service you want ChatGPT-5 to interact with, such as a weather API or a CRM system.

2. **Authentication**: Use API keys or tokens to securely connect.
3. **Define the requests**: Decide which endpoints you want to call and what parameters they require.
4. **Process the responses**: ChatGPT-5 receives structured data, interprets it, and integrates it into the conversation.
5. **Output the result**: Present the information to the user in a clear and usable format.

4. Example Scenarios

- **Customer Support**: Connect to a ticketing system's API so the model can retrieve and update customer service requests.
- **E-commerce**: Integrate with inventory APIs to show available products and complete orders.
- **Finance**: Connect to market data APIs to analyze trends and provide investment insights.
- **IoT Devices**: Control smart home systems via device control APIs.

5. Best Practices

- Ensure the API you are connecting to is secure and reliable.
- Validate and sanitize all input and output to avoid incorrect or unsafe operations.
- Respect rate limits and usage terms to prevent service disruptions.
- Provide clear prompts that define exactly what the model should request from the API.

Why This Matters

Connecting ChatGPT-5 to APIs elevates its capabilities beyond standalone text generation. It can interact with the outside world, perform real-time tasks, and seamlessly integrate into business, research, and personal workflows. This makes the model a practical tool for automation, data retrieval, and operational efficiency.

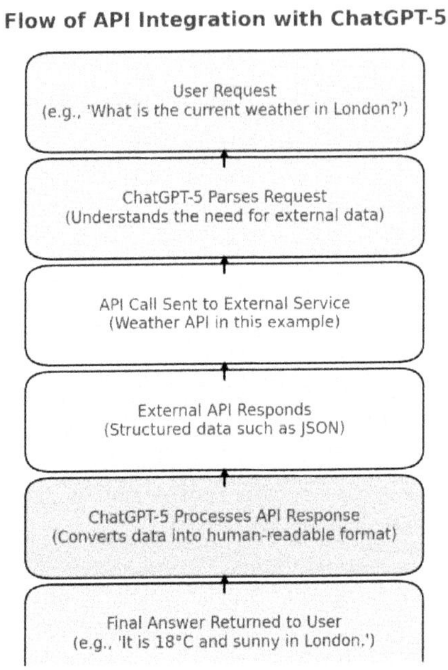

Embedding ChatGPT-5 into Apps and Workflows

Embedding ChatGPT-5 into applications and workflows transforms it from a standalone conversational system into a fully integrated component of business operations, creative tools, or customer-facing platforms. This enables the model to deliver intelligent assistance directly where it is needed, without requiring users to switch between different environments.

1. What It Means to Embed ChatGPT-5

Embedding refers to integrating ChatGPT-5's functionality within existing software, mobile applications, or automated systems so it works as part of the native user experience. Instead of accessing

ChatGPT-5 on a separate website, users can interact with it directly in the tool they are already using.

2. Benefits of Embedding into Apps and Workflows

- **Seamless user experience**: Eliminates the need to leave the current platform to access AI capabilities.
- **Time savings**: Reduces manual steps in processes by automating parts of the workflow.
- **Custom functionality**: The integration can be tailored to specific industries or use cases.
- **Real-time responses**: Provides instant assistance without delay between switching applications.

3. Common Embedding Scenarios

- **Customer Service Platforms**: Adding ChatGPT-5 as a live assistant in a customer support dashboard to help agents respond faster.
- **Document Editing Tools**: Embedding ChatGPT-5 to help draft, summarize, or improve text directly inside a word processor.
- **E-commerce Websites**: Using ChatGPT-5 as a shopping assistant that recommends products and answers questions in real time.
- **Business Analytics Tools**: Allowing users to query data in plain language and receive instant visual or textual analysis.

4. How the Embedding Process Works

1. **Identify integration points**: Determine where in the app or workflow ChatGPT-5 can provide the most value.

2. **Connect via API or SDK**: Use OpenAI's API or third-party development kits to link the model to your platform.
3. **Design the interaction flow**: Map out how users will trigger and interact with the model.
4. **Customize behavior**: Apply prompt templates, role instructions, or domain-specific data for targeted responses.
5. **Test and refine**: Ensure the integration meets user needs and maintains accuracy.

5. Best Practices

- Keep interactions context-aware so the model remembers relevant details throughout the session.
- Ensure security and privacy compliance when embedding into systems that handle sensitive information.
- Monitor performance and gather feedback to improve the integration over time.
- Offer clear onboarding for users so they understand how to interact with the embedded AI.

Why This Matters

Embedding ChatGPT-5 into apps and workflows turns AI from a separate tool into an integral part of daily operations. This results in faster decision-making, higher productivity, and better user engagement. The model becomes a silent but powerful collaborator that works in the background, enhancing every interaction.

Embedding ChatGPT-5 into Applications and Workflows

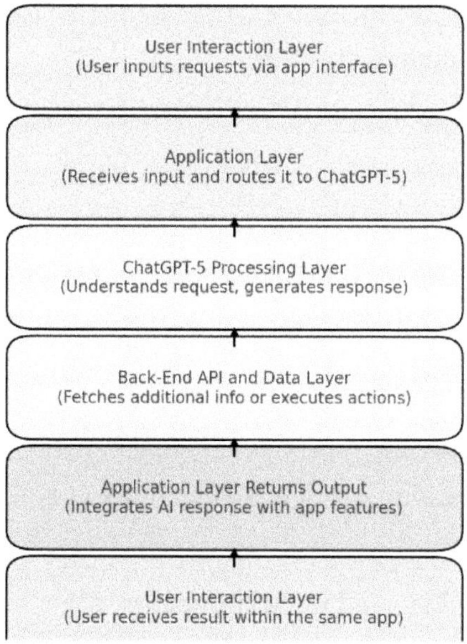

Using Plugins and External Tools

Plugins and external tools extend the capabilities of ChatGPT-5 far beyond its built-in features. By integrating specialized services, data sources, and processing modules, the model can perform tasks that require specific domain knowledge, access to real-time information, or the ability to interact with third-party systems.

1. What Plugins and External Tools Are

A plugin is an add-on that connects ChatGPT-5 to an external service or database, enabling it to perform specific functions it cannot do on its own. External tools can include analytical software, automation platforms, content creation suites, or industry-specific applications that work alongside ChatGPT-5 to enhance its output.

2. Benefits of Using Plugins and External Tools

- **Real-time access**: Enables ChatGPT-5 to retrieve up-to-date data such as live sports scores, stock prices, or breaking news.

- **Specialized functionality**: Allows access to niche capabilities like medical knowledge bases, legal document search, or coding libraries.
- **Automation**: Connects ChatGPT-5 to tools that handle repetitive tasks such as scheduling, file conversions, or batch processing.
- **Improved accuracy**: Supplements ChatGPT-5's general knowledge with targeted and verified sources.

3. Common Use Cases

- **Travel planning**: A travel plugin can provide flight options, hotel availability, and local attractions in real time.
- **E-commerce support**: Plugins can check product stock, process orders, and track shipments.
- **Data analysis**: External analytical tools can process large datasets and return summarized insights through ChatGPT-5.
- **Content creation**: Creative tools can generate images, videos, or music based on prompts from ChatGPT-5.

4. How the Process Works

1. **Identify the need**: Decide what task or feature requires a plugin or external tool.
2. **Select the right plugin/tool**: Choose a trusted and compatible option that meets your requirements.
3. **Enable or install**: Activate the plugin within ChatGPT-5's settings or connect it via an API.
4. **Interact through prompts**: Use conversational commands to request information or actions from the connected tool.

5. **Receive and review results**: The response is returned through ChatGPT-5 in a user-friendly format.

5. Best Practices

- Verify the credibility and security of plugins and external tools before using them.
- Use clear and specific prompts to maximize the benefit of the integration.
- Monitor plugin performance and disable tools that are outdated or unreliable.
- Combine multiple plugins where possible to create more powerful workflows.

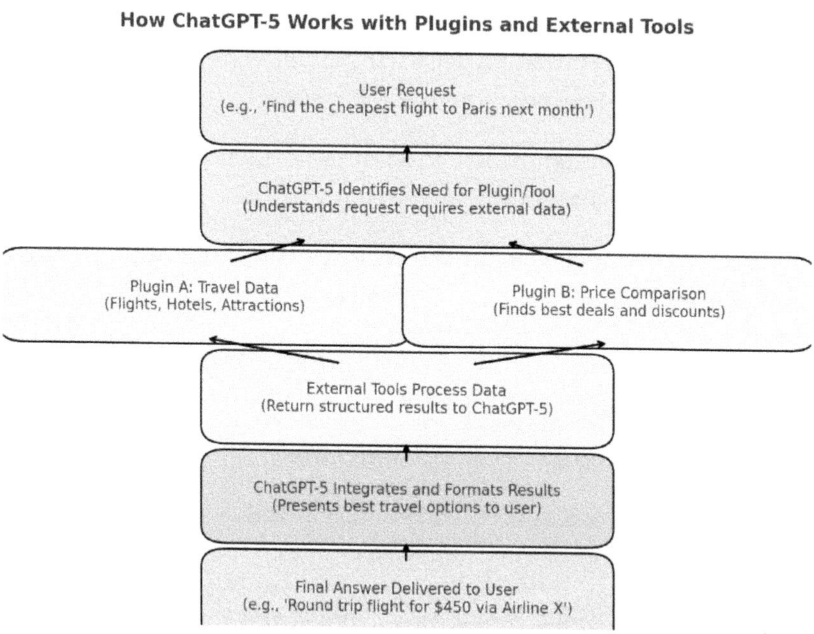

Part III: Specialized Applications

Chapter 10 – Business and Professional Use

Customer Service

ChatGPT-5 offers significant value in the customer service sector by providing fast, consistent, and accurate support to clients. It can serve as a first line of assistance, handle repetitive inquiries, and escalate complex issues to human agents when necessary. With its advanced natural language understanding, ChatGPT-5 can interpret diverse customer requests and deliver tailored responses that match the tone and context of the conversation.

1. Benefits of Using ChatGPT-5 for Customer Service

- **24/7 availability**: Provides continuous support without staffing limitations.
- **Scalability**: Can handle thousands of queries simultaneously, reducing wait times.
- **Consistency**: Delivers standardized responses to maintain brand voice and policy adherence.
- **Cost efficiency**: Reduces the need for large human support teams while improving customer satisfaction.

2. Common Customer Service Applications

- **Live chat assistance**: Responds instantly to customer queries on websites or apps.
- **Ticket triaging**: Categorizes and prioritizes incoming requests for human agents.
- **FAQ automation**: Answers common questions without human intervention.

- **Multi-language support**: Communicates with customers in different languages, expanding global reach.

3. How It Works in Practice

1. **Customer initiates contact**: A customer sends a query through a live chat widget, email, or social media.
2. **ChatGPT-5 processes the message**: The model identifies the intent, urgency, and key details.
3. **Automated response or escalation**: The system either provides a direct solution or forwards the issue to a support agent.
4. **Follow-up**: The model can check if the customer is satisfied or requires further assistance.

4. Best Practices for Implementation

- Integrate ChatGPT-5 with your CRM and ticketing systems for seamless operations.
- Provide the model with company-specific training or fine-tuning to align with brand standards.
- Set clear guidelines for when to escalate to human support.
- Monitor responses regularly to ensure quality and compliance.

Why This Matters

Customer service is one of the most impactful areas for AI integration. By using ChatGPT-5, businesses can improve response times, maintain high service standards, and free up human agents to focus on more complex tasks. This not only enhances customer satisfaction but also increases operational efficiency.

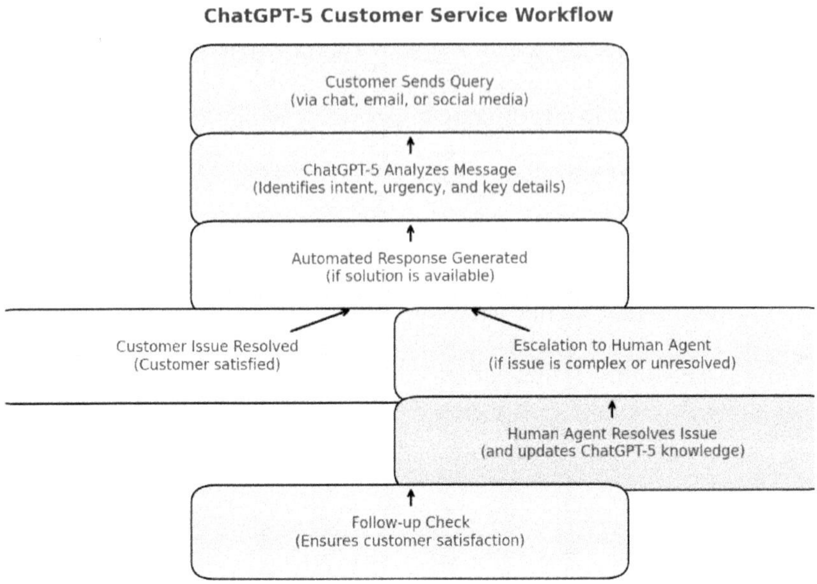

Marketing and Content Creation

ChatGPT-5 plays an increasingly important role in marketing and content creation by helping businesses produce high-quality, relevant, and engaging material at scale. Its ability to understand brand tone, target audiences, and diverse content formats makes it an effective partner for marketing teams and creative professionals.

1. Benefits of Using ChatGPT-5 for Marketing and Content Creation

- **Faster content production**: Generates copy, captions, and articles quickly, reducing turnaround times.
- **Consistency in brand voice**: Maintains a unified style across multiple platforms and campaigns.
- **Cost efficiency**: Reduces the need for extensive writing teams while maintaining quality output.

- **Idea generation**: Provides fresh perspectives and creative suggestions for campaigns and stories.

2. Common Applications

- **Social media posts**: Creates captions, hashtags, and short-form content optimized for engagement.
- **Email campaigns**: Drafts personalized marketing emails tailored to different customer segments.
- **Blog articles**: Produces informative and SEO-friendly posts that attract and retain audiences.
- **Ad copywriting**: Crafts compelling advertisements that resonate with target demographics.
- **Video scripts**: Writes outlines and dialogue for promotional videos, tutorials, and product launches.

3. How It Works in Practice

1. **Define the objective**: Identify whether the content is meant to inform, persuade, or entertain.
2. **Provide brand guidelines**: Include tone, style, keywords, and any must-have phrases.
3. **Generate the draft**: ChatGPT-5 produces the initial version of the content.
4. **Refine and customize**: Adjust for accuracy, local relevance, and brand alignment.
5. **Deploy and monitor**: Publish the content and track its performance to guide future improvements.

4. Best Practices for Implementation

- Use clear prompts that specify the target audience, purpose, and tone.
- Pair AI-generated drafts with human editing for maximum impact.
- Regularly review output to ensure it aligns with marketing goals.
- Experiment with different creative approaches to see what resonates best with the audience.

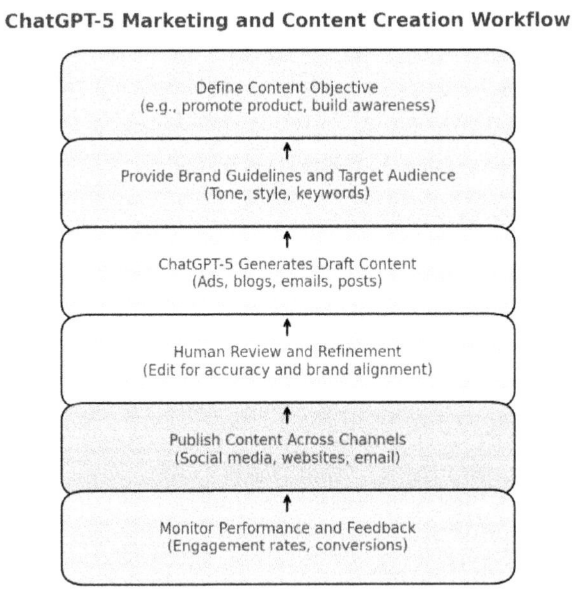

Data Analysis and Research Assistance

ChatGPT-5 has become a valuable partner for professionals and organizations that need to interpret data and conduct research efficiently. By combining advanced language understanding with the ability to process structured and unstructured information, it can assist in everything from summarizing complex reports to generating actionable insights from large datasets.

1. Benefits of Using ChatGPT-5 for Data Analysis and Research

- **Speed and efficiency**: Processes large volumes of information much faster than manual methods.
- **Enhanced interpretation**: Explains technical results in clear, accessible language for decision-makers.
- **Pattern recognition**: Identifies trends and correlations in datasets that might be missed by human review.
- **Versatile research support**: Works with a variety of data types including text, numerical data, and multimedia sources.

2. Common Applications

- **Market research**: Summarizes competitor activities, consumer behavior, and industry trends.
- **Survey analysis**: Aggregates and interprets survey responses to reveal patterns.
- **Financial analysis**: Reviews financial statements, identifies key metrics, and predicts possible outcomes.
- **Scientific literature review**: Synthesizes findings from multiple academic sources into a concise summary.
- **Data visualization assistance**: Suggests or creates charts, graphs, and tables to present results effectively.

3. How It Works in Practice

1. **Data input**: The user provides datasets, documents, or URLs containing relevant information.

2. **Processing and organization**: ChatGPT-5 categorizes and structures the data for easier analysis.
3. **Insight generation**: The model identifies key points, patterns, and anomalies.
4. **Reporting**: Results are compiled into summaries, detailed reports, or presentations.
5. **Follow-up queries**: Users can refine questions to explore deeper insights or new directions.

4. Best Practices for Implementation

- Provide clear instructions about the desired format, level of detail, and focus areas.
- Use verified data sources to maintain accuracy and reliability.
- Combine AI-generated insights with human expertise to validate conclusions.
- Integrate ChatGPT-5 with analytics tools for more advanced statistical processing.

Why This Matters

Data analysis and research are time-consuming but essential parts of business decision-making. ChatGPT-5 streamlines these tasks, allowing professionals to focus on strategy rather than manual processing. By turning complex data into understandable insights, it helps organizations make faster and more informed choices.

ChatGPT-5 Data Analysis and Research Workflow

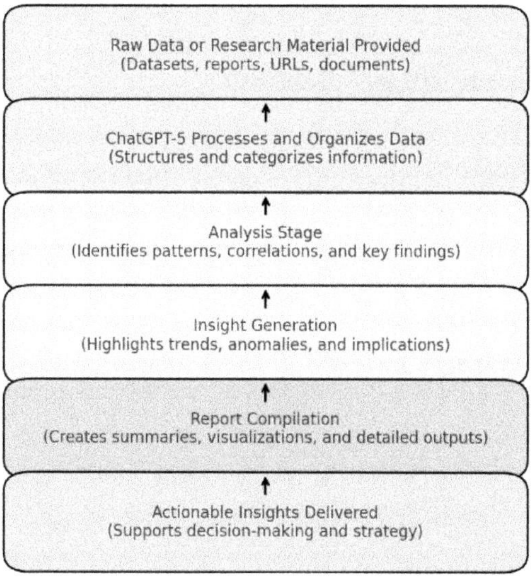

Chapter 11 – Education and Learning

Tutoring and Concept Explanation

ChatGPT-5 is increasingly being used as a personalized tutor and knowledge assistant in education. It can explain complex topics in simple terms, adapt its explanations to the learner's level, and provide interactive exercises to reinforce understanding. This makes it a valuable tool for students, educators, and lifelong learners.

1. Benefits of Using ChatGPT-5 for Tutoring and Concept Explanation

- **Personalized learning**: Adjusts explanations based on the learner's background knowledge and pace.
- **Availability**: Offers assistance at any time, enabling learning outside of traditional classroom hours.
- **Wide subject coverage**: Supports topics across science, mathematics, humanities, technology, and more.
- **Interactivity**: Engages learners with questions, quizzes, and scenario-based exercises.

2. Common Applications

- **Homework help**: Guides students through problem-solving rather than simply giving the answer.
- **Exam preparation**: Provides summaries, flashcards, and practice questions for specific subjects.
- **Concept clarification**: Breaks down difficult theories or formulas into step-by-step explanations.
- **Language learning**: Offers grammar corrections, vocabulary expansion, and conversational practice.

3. How It Works in Practice

1. **Student asks a question**: The learner types or speaks a question or topic they need help with.
2. **ChatGPT-5 analyzes the query**: Identifies the key concept, the learner's level, and the best explanation style.
3. **Response generation**: Provides a detailed explanation, including examples, analogies, or visual aids.
4. **Follow-up interaction**: Answers further questions or adjusts explanations based on feedback.
5. **Reinforcement**: Supplies exercises or quizzes to help solidify the knowledge.

4. Best Practices for Implementation

- Encourage students to ask follow-up questions for deeper understanding.
- Use ChatGPT-5 alongside traditional resources such as textbooks and lectures.
- Verify complex or critical information with trusted educational materials.
- Apply context-specific prompts to get tailored, relevant explanations.

Why This Matters
Effective learning depends on clear explanations, timely feedback, and opportunities for practice. ChatGPT-5 provides these elements in a flexible and scalable way, empowering learners to grasp challenging concepts and build confidence in their abilities.

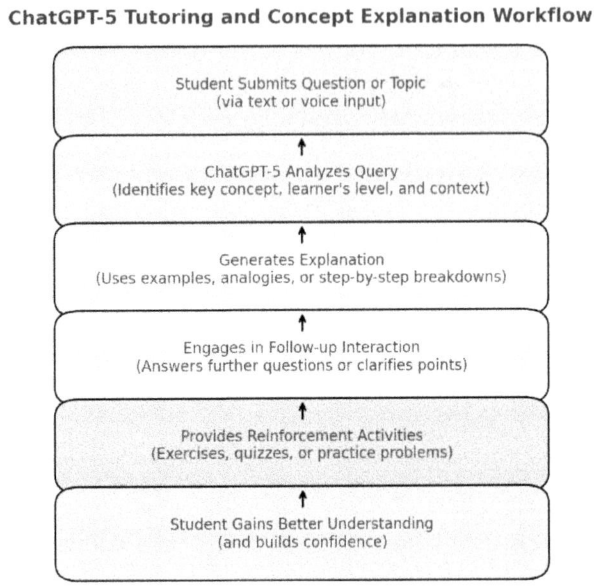

Language Learning

ChatGPT-5 serves as a highly adaptable and interactive companion for individuals seeking to learn new languages or improve existing skills. Its ability to understand, generate, and correct text in multiple languages makes it valuable for both self-directed learners and classroom environments. By simulating natural conversations, offering grammar feedback, and providing vocabulary practice, ChatGPT-5 supports learners in developing fluency and confidence.

1. Benefits of Using ChatGPT-5 for Language Learning

- **Conversational practice**: Engages in realistic dialogues that help learners apply their knowledge in context.
- **Immediate feedback**: Corrects grammar, spelling, and sentence structure in real time.
- **Multilingual versatility**: Supports a wide range of languages, allowing learners to switch between them easily.

- **Adaptive learning**: Adjusts difficulty and complexity based on the learner's proficiency level.

2. Common Applications

- **Dialogue simulation**: Practices common scenarios such as ordering food, making travel arrangements, or attending meetings.
- **Grammar coaching**: Explains rules and offers examples for correct usage.
- **Vocabulary building**: Introduces new words, phrases, and idioms in context.
- **Pronunciation guidance**: When paired with text-to-speech tools, offers spoken examples for practice.
- **Cultural context**: Shares idiomatic expressions and cultural references to enhance communication skills.

3. How It Works in Practice

1. **Learner initiates a session**: The student specifies the language and type of practice they want.
2. **Interactive exchange**: ChatGPT-5 responds in the target language, encouraging the learner to participate actively.
3. **Feedback and correction**: The model identifies errors and provides corrected sentences with explanations.
4. **Vocabulary reinforcement**: Words or phrases introduced are repeated in later interactions to strengthen retention.
5. **Progress tracking**: Learners can request summaries of mistakes, improvements, and suggested focus areas.

4. Best Practices for Implementation

- Use a mix of casual conversation and structured exercises.
- Request cultural notes to better understand idioms and context-specific usage.
- Combine ChatGPT-5 practice with listening and speaking exercises through audio tools.
- Gradually increase the complexity of prompts to match skill growth.

Why This Matters

Language learning requires consistent practice, varied exposure, and meaningful feedback. ChatGPT-5 delivers all three in a flexible and engaging way, helping learners move beyond memorization into genuine communication skills.

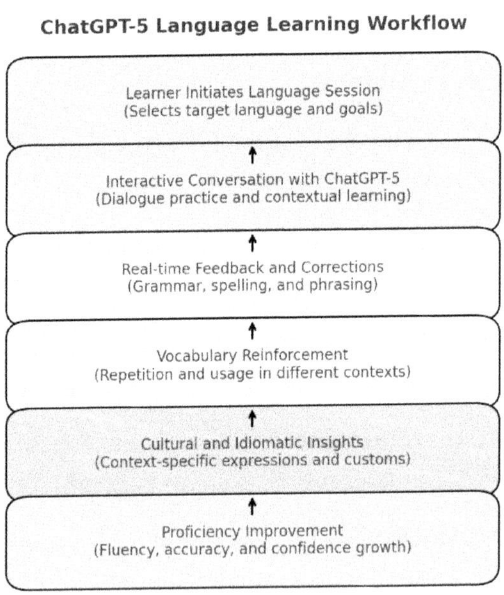

Personalized Study Plans

ChatGPT-5 can act as a powerful assistant for creating and managing personalized study plans that adapt to a learner's goals, pace, and progress. By considering individual strengths, weaknesses, and available time, it can design structured schedules that optimize learning efficiency and keep the student motivated.

1. Benefits of Using ChatGPT-5 for Personalized Study Plans

- **Custom scheduling**: Creates study plans based on the learner's availability and deadlines.
- **Adaptive progression**: Adjusts the plan as the learner's skills improve or if challenges arise.
- **Balanced workload**: Distributes topics and exercises evenly to prevent burnout.
- **Goal-oriented structure**: Aligns learning activities with short-term and long-term objectives.

2. Common Applications

- **Exam preparation**: Breaks down the syllabus into manageable daily or weekly segments.
- **Skill development**: Organizes learning for new abilities such as coding, writing, or public speaking.
- **Language learning schedules**: Balances vocabulary, grammar, reading, listening, and speaking tasks.
- **Professional certification training**: Outlines study paths for industry-specific qualifications.

3. How It Works in Practice

1. **Goal setting**: The learner specifies their subject, target proficiency, and completion date.

2. **Assessment**: ChatGPT-5 asks questions or uses provided results to gauge current knowledge level.
3. **Plan creation**: Generates a structured schedule with milestones, resources, and practice tasks.
4. **Monitoring progress**: Checks in periodically to assess how well the learner is keeping pace.
5. **Adjustments**: Modifies the schedule if the learner is ahead or behind, or if new priorities emerge.

4. Best Practices for Implementation

- Be clear and specific about time availability and target outcomes.
- Include both study and rest periods to ensure balance.
- Combine AI-generated schedules with trusted resources such as textbooks and expert-led classes.
- Review progress regularly and refine the plan to stay aligned with goals.

Why This Matters

A well-structured study plan keeps learners focused, organized, and accountable. ChatGPT-5 makes it possible to create these plans quickly and adjust them dynamically, ensuring that every learner receives a roadmap tailored to their personal needs and circumstances.

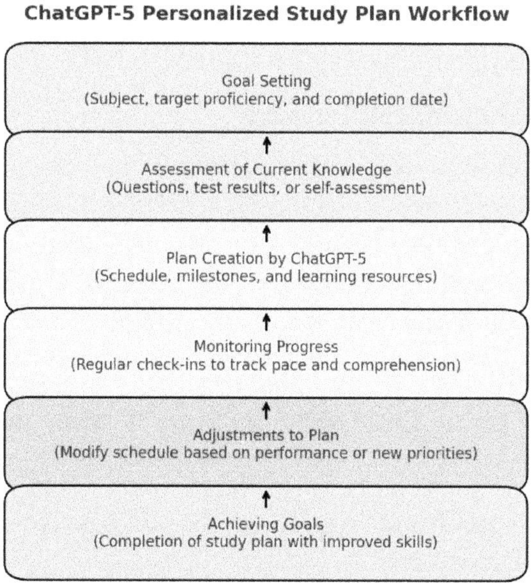
ChatGPT-5 Personalized Study Plan Workflow
Goal Setting
(Subject, target proficiency, and completion date)
Assessment of Current Knowledge
(Questions, test results, or self-assessment)
Plan Creation by ChatGPT-5
(Schedule, milestones, and learning resources)
Monitoring Progress
(Regular check-ins to track pace and comprehension)
Adjustments to Plan
(Modify schedule based on performance or new priorities)
Achieving Goals
(Completion of study plan with improved skills)

Chapter 12 – Creative and Artistic Applications

Story Writing and World Building

ChatGPT-5 can serve as a creative partner for authors, game designers, and screenwriters who need assistance in generating stories, designing fictional worlds, or expanding narrative ideas. Its ability to understand themes, genres, and character dynamics allows it to produce consistent, imaginative, and engaging content that matches the creator's vision.

1. Benefits of Using ChatGPT-5 for Story Writing and World Building

- **Idea generation**: Suggests unique plot concepts, settings, and character arcs.
- **Consistency**: Maintains continuity of characters, timelines, and world rules across long narratives.
- **Speed**: Produces detailed descriptions and dialogue quickly, reducing initial drafting time.
- **Flexibility**: Adapts writing style to match specific genres, tones, or target audiences.

2. Common Applications

- **Novel and short story development**: Generates plot outlines, chapters, and character dialogues.
- **Game design**: Creates immersive lore, quests, and world mechanics for role-playing games.
- **Screenwriting**: Assists with scene creation, pacing, and script formatting.
- **World-building detail**: Develops cultures, geography, history, and political systems for fictional settings.

3. How It Works in Practice

1. **Concept input**: The creator provides a theme, genre, and any key ideas or constraints.
2. **Story framework creation**: ChatGPT-5 generates outlines, character profiles, and setting descriptions.
3. **Iterative refinement**: The creator requests changes, adds details, or adjusts tone.
4. **Expanded content generation**: Produces dialogue, narration, and action sequences that fit the established framework.
5. **Final polishing**: Ensures coherence, style consistency, and alignment with the creator's goals.

4. Best Practices for Implementation

- Provide detailed prompts with clear parameters for setting, plot, and character traits.
- Use ChatGPT-5 for brainstorming and drafting while reserving final editing for human judgment.
- Maintain a separate reference file for key details to ensure consistency in world building.
- Experiment with different prompt styles to inspire new creative directions.

Why This Matters
Story writing and world building require both imagination and structure. ChatGPT-5 accelerates the creative process by offering a steady stream of ideas and filling in descriptive details, while still allowing human creators to maintain full creative control.

ChatGPT-5 Story Writing and World Building Workflow

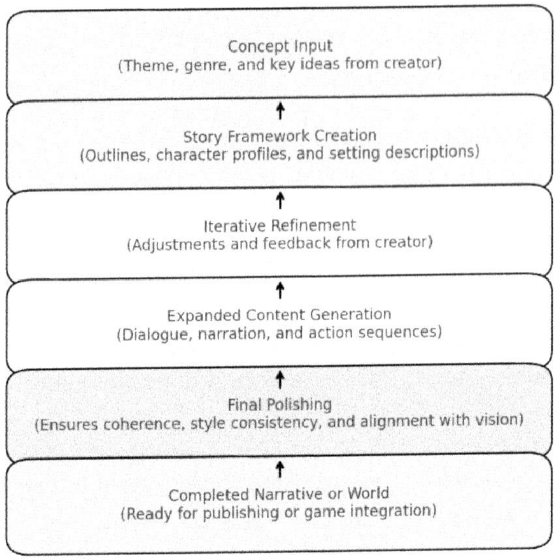

Poetry, Lyrics, and Scripts

ChatGPT-5 can assist writers, musicians, and playwrights in creating original works such as poems, song lyrics, and scripts. Its advanced language capabilities allow it to work with diverse styles, themes, and formats, making it an adaptable partner for artistic expression. By understanding rhythm, rhyme, tone, and dramatic structure, ChatGPT-5 can produce creative drafts that artists can refine into finished works.

1. Benefits of Using ChatGPT-5 for Poetry, Lyrics, and Scripts

- **Versatility**: Can adapt to a variety of genres, from romantic poetry to satirical lyrics and dramatic plays.
- **Speed of idea generation**: Offers rapid brainstorming and first-draft creation.
- **Stylistic mimicry**: Can emulate the tone and style of specific poets, lyricists, or playwrights.

- **Collaborative refinement**: Enables iterative feedback loops to fine-tune the creative output.

2. Common Applications

- **Poetry**: Generates verses in free verse, sonnet form, haiku, or other structures.
- **Song lyrics**: Writes verses, choruses, and bridges aligned with a chosen mood or genre.
- **Scripts**: Produces stage plays, film screenplays, or radio drama scripts with dialogue and scene directions.
- **Creative exercises**: Offers writing prompts and unfinished pieces for artistic development.

3. How It Works in Practice

1. **Creative brief**: The artist provides details such as theme, mood, genre, and any structural requirements.
2. **Initial draft generation**: ChatGPT-5 creates a complete draft based on the provided guidelines.
3. **Feedback and editing**: The creator reviews the draft and suggests changes to tone, pacing, or structure.
4. **Refinement stage**: ChatGPT-5 incorporates the feedback, adjusting style and word choice.
5. **Final output**: The work is ready for performance, recording, or publication after human review.

4. Best Practices for Implementation

- Provide explicit instructions on tone, length, and structure.
- Use ChatGPT-5 as a creative starting point, not as a final authority on artistic decisions.

- Combine AI-generated lines with personal edits to ensure authenticity.
- Explore multiple drafts and variations before deciding on the final piece.

Why This Matters
Artistic expression often requires a blend of inspiration, technical skill, and refinement. ChatGPT-5 accelerates the early creative stages, offering multiple stylistic options while leaving room for human emotion and craftsmanship to shape the final work.

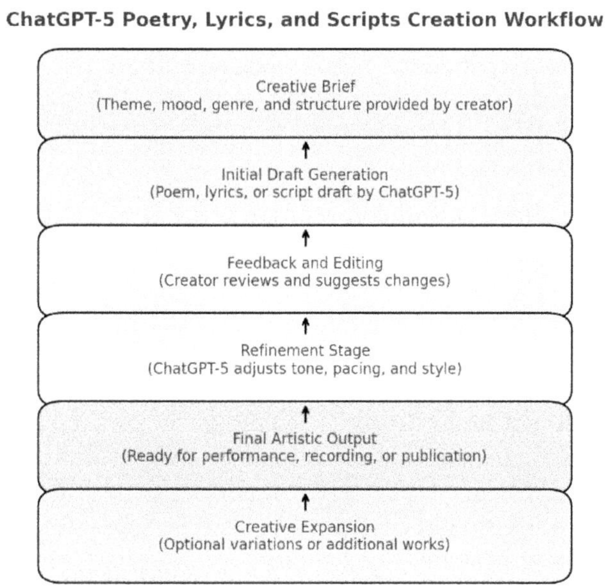

Visual Art Collaboration

ChatGPT-5 can work as a creative collaborator for visual artists, designers, and illustrators by helping them conceptualize ideas, refine artistic directions, and even guide the process of generating AI-assisted images. While it cannot replace the creative touch of a human artist, it serves as a powerful partner for brainstorming, planning, and executing visual concepts.

1. Benefits of Using ChatGPT-5 for Visual Art Collaboration

- **Concept development**: Transforms vague ideas into clear and actionable artistic concepts.
- **Stylistic diversity**: Suggests themes and visual styles ranging from realism to abstract expression.
- **Integration with other tools**: Works alongside image generation models and design software to produce visual drafts.
- **Creative problem solving**: Proposes new ways to visualize ideas or adapt them for different audiences.

2. Common Applications

- **Illustration planning**: Outlines composition, subject matter, and mood before the artist begins sketching.
- **Graphic design support**: Suggests layouts, typography styles, and color palettes for branding or promotional materials.
- **Concept art for games and films**: Helps in world design, character visualization, and environmental scenes.
- **Mixed media inspiration**: Proposes ways to combine photography, painting, and digital effects.

3. How It Works in Practice

1. **Idea sharing**: The artist provides an initial concept, theme, or visual reference.

2. **Concept expansion**: ChatGPT-5 refines the idea with detailed scene descriptions, style suggestions, and thematic enhancements.
3. **Visual translation**: Works with AI art tools or human artists to turn the concept into sketches or drafts.
4. **Iterative refinement**: Adjusts elements such as lighting, perspective, or color based on feedback.
5. **Finalization**: Produces a polished artwork ready for exhibition, publishing, or integration into larger projects.

4. Best Practices for Implementation

- Provide clear descriptions of the intended mood, style, and purpose.
- Use ChatGPT-5 as a brainstorming and refinement tool, not as the sole creative authority.
- Combine AI suggestions with personal artistic intuition.
- Experiment with different prompt structures to explore unexpected artistic directions.

Why This Matters

Visual art thrives on inspiration, experimentation, and iteration. ChatGPT-5 enhances these processes by providing rapid ideation, stylistic guidance, and conceptual depth, enabling artists to explore more creative possibilities in less time.

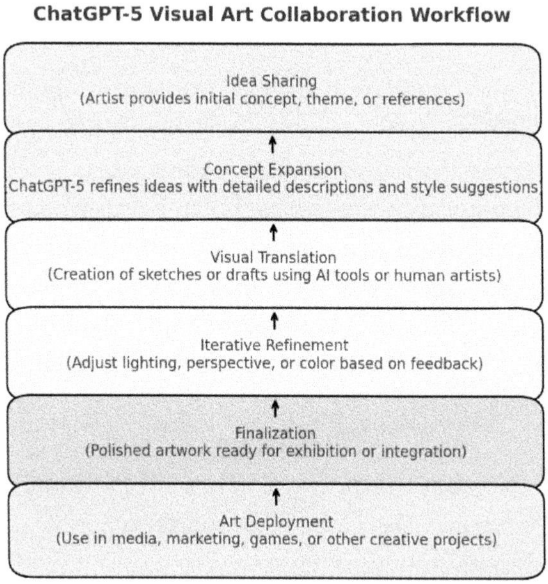
ChatGPT-5 Visual Art Collaboration Workflow
Idea Sharing
(Artist provides initial concept, theme, or references)
Concept Expansion
(ChatGPT-5 refines ideas with detailed descriptions and style suggestions)
Visual Translation
(Creation of sketches or drafts using AI tools or human artists)
Iterative Refinement
(Adjust lighting, perspective, or color based on feedback)
Finalization
(Polished artwork ready for exhibition or integration)
Art Deployment
(Use in media, marketing, games, or other creative projects)

Chapter 13 – Technical and Research Applications

Coding Assistance

ChatGPT-5 serves as a highly capable coding assistant for developers, students, and technical professionals. It can help with writing, understanding, debugging, and optimizing code in multiple programming languages. With its deep contextual understanding and ability to process natural language instructions, ChatGPT-5 bridges the gap between human intent and precise code implementation.

1. Benefits of Using ChatGPT-5 for Coding Assistance

- **Multi-language support**: Works with Python, JavaScript, Java, C++, HTML, CSS, SQL, and more.
- **Code generation**: Transforms natural language requests into fully functional code snippets or scripts.
- **Debugging support**: Identifies syntax errors, logical mistakes, and potential performance issues.
- **Optimization**: Suggests ways to make code more efficient, readable, and maintainable.

2. Common Applications

- **Learning to code**: Explains programming concepts, algorithms, and data structures in simple terms.
- **Rapid prototyping**: Creates quick code drafts for testing ideas before full-scale development.
- **Automation scripts**: Generates scripts for repetitive tasks, such as data processing or file management.
- **API integration**: Produces example code for connecting to and working with third-party APIs.

3. How It Works in Practice

1. **User query**: The developer describes the problem, task, or desired feature in natural language.
2. **Code generation**: ChatGPT-5 writes the requested code in the chosen language.
3. **Review and feedback**: The user tests the code, provides feedback, or asks for improvements.
4. **Refinement**: ChatGPT-5 updates the code to meet functional, performance, or style requirements.
5. **Explanation**: Provides step-by-step explanations for how the code works, helping users learn while building.

4. Best Practices for Implementation

- Always test AI-generated code before deploying it in production environments.
- Provide detailed specifications and examples in your request to improve accuracy.
- Use ChatGPT-5 as a supplement to, not a replacement for, human code review.
- Leverage its explanation capabilities to improve your own programming skills.

Why This Matters

Coding can be time-consuming, especially when tackling unfamiliar syntax, complex algorithms, or tricky bugs. ChatGPT-5 accelerates development by providing immediate, context-aware coding support while also acting as an interactive tutor for continuous skill improvement.

ChatGPT-5 Coding Assistance Workflow

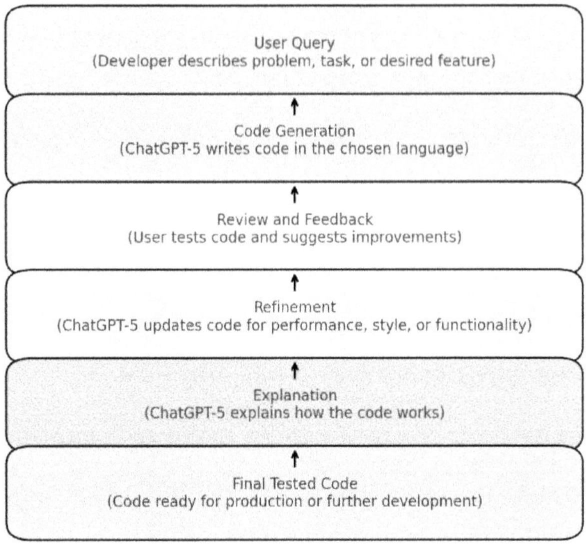

Scientific Paper Summarization

ChatGPT-5 can assist researchers, academics, and students by summarizing complex scientific papers into clear and concise formats. This helps users quickly understand key findings, methodologies, and implications without reading the full document in detail. Its ability to process dense technical language and extract essential points makes it a valuable research companion.

1. Benefits of Using ChatGPT-5 for Scientific Paper Summarization

- **Time efficiency**: Saves hours of reading by distilling papers into short, informative summaries.
- **Clarity**: Translates technical jargon into accessible language for broader audiences.
- **Focus on essentials**: Highlights key findings, hypotheses, methods, and conclusions.

- **Adaptability**: Can produce summaries tailored for experts, students, or the general public.

2. Common Applications

- **Literature reviews**: Summarizes multiple papers to identify trends and research gaps.
- **Research collaboration**: Provides quick overviews for team members with different areas of expertise.
- **Grant applications**: Helps condense prior work into digestible summaries for funding proposals.
- **Public science communication**: Produces layman-friendly explanations for broader dissemination.

3. How It Works in Practice

1. **Paper input**: The user provides a scientific paper or its text.
2. **Key element identification**: ChatGPT-5 extracts important sections such as objectives, methods, results, and discussion.
3. **Condensed summary generation**: Produces a concise summary tailored to the user's preferred level of detail.
4. **Optional simplification**: Converts the summary into plain language for non-specialist audiences.
5. **Review and refinement**: The user checks for accuracy and requests adjustments if needed.

4. Best Practices for Implementation

- Provide the full text or detailed excerpts for more accurate summaries.
- Indicate the desired length and complexity of the summary.

- Verify the extracted information against the original paper to avoid misinterpretation.
- Use AI summaries as a starting point, not as a substitute for reading important studies in depth.

Why This Matters
Scientific progress relies on understanding existing research. ChatGPT-5 accelerates this process by breaking down complex studies into clear insights, making it easier for researchers and students to stay informed and focus on advancing their own work.

ChatGPT-5 Scientific Paper Summarization Workflow

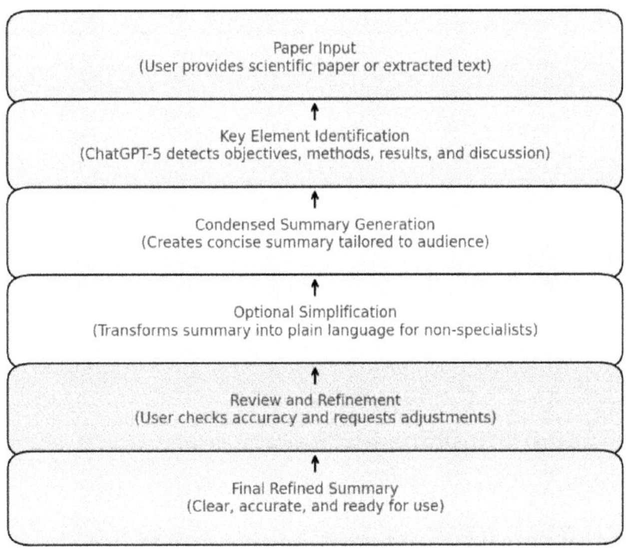

Hypothesis Generation

ChatGPT-5 can assist researchers and innovators by helping them generate testable hypotheses across various disciplines, from biomedical science to social research and engineering. Its strength lies in rapidly processing large amounts of information, recognizing patterns, and suggesting logical connections that might form the basis of new investigations.

1. Benefits of Using ChatGPT-5 for Hypothesis Generation

- **Speed**: Produces multiple plausible hypotheses in a fraction of the time compared to traditional brainstorming.
- **Breadth of knowledge**: Draws from a wide variety of domains to suggest interdisciplinary ideas.
- **Pattern recognition**: Identifies correlations and potential causal relationships from given data or literature summaries.
- **Creativity**: Offers unconventional ideas that can spark innovative research directions.

2. Common Applications

- **Scientific research**: Generates hypotheses for laboratory experiments or field studies.
- **Product development**: Suggests potential design improvements based on user feedback and market data.
- **Social science studies**: Proposes research questions related to human behavior, economics, or cultural trends.
- **Engineering projects**: Identifies areas where performance, safety, or efficiency could be improved.

3. How It Works in Practice

1. **Input data or literature**: The researcher provides relevant studies, datasets, or background information.
2. **Pattern and gap analysis**: ChatGPT-5 highlights underexplored areas or interesting relationships.

3. **Hypothesis proposal**: Produces one or more testable statements based on the identified patterns.
4. **Feasibility check**: Researcher evaluates whether the hypotheses are practical, ethical, and within resource constraints.
5. **Refinement**: Hypotheses are fine-tuned for clarity, specificity, and testability.

4. Best Practices for Implementation

- Clearly define the research scope and objectives before asking for hypotheses.
- Provide as much context and relevant data as possible to improve quality.
- Use ChatGPT-5 suggestions as starting points and validate them with expert review.
- Be prepared to refine and reject ideas that are not feasible or scientifically sound.

Why This Matters

The ability to quickly formulate and evaluate hypotheses is essential for accelerating the research cycle. ChatGPT-5 enhances this process by combining speed, breadth of knowledge, and creative thinking, enabling researchers to explore more possibilities in less time.

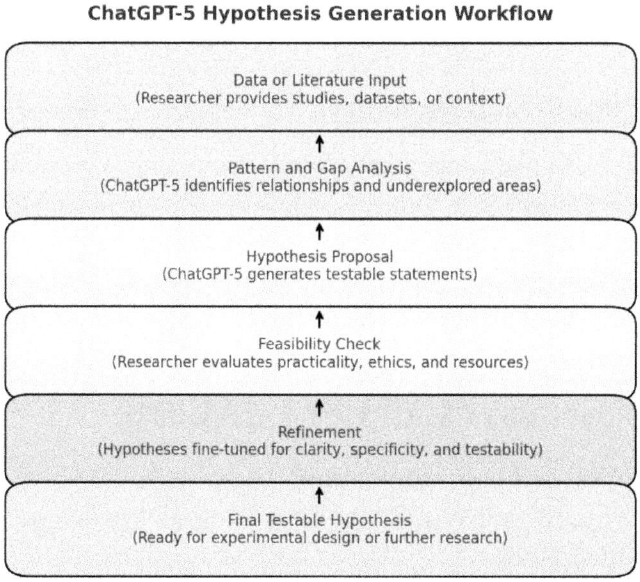
ChatGPT-5 Hypothesis Generation Workflow
Data or Literature Input
(Researcher provides studies, datasets, or context)
Pattern and Gap Analysis
(ChatGPT-5 identifies relationships and underexplored areas)
Hypothesis Proposal
(ChatGPT-5 generates testable statements)
Feasibility Check
(Researcher evaluates practicality, ethics, and resources)
Refinement
(Hypotheses fine-tuned for clarity, specificity, and testability)
Final Testable Hypothesis
(Ready for experimental design or further research)

Chapter 14 – Accessibility and Inclusion

Helping People with Disabilities

ChatGPT-5 can play a significant role in improving accessibility and inclusion for individuals with disabilities by offering personalized assistance, adaptive communication tools, and support for independent living. Its ability to process and generate text, speech, and visual content allows it to be integrated into solutions that break down barriers to information, education, and everyday tasks.

1. Benefits of Using ChatGPT-5 for Accessibility

- **Enhanced communication**: Assists individuals with speech or hearing impairments by converting spoken language to text and vice versa.
- **Information accessibility**: Summarizes and simplifies complex information for users with cognitive disabilities.
- **Visual assistance**: Works with image recognition tools to describe surroundings or read printed text for individuals with visual impairments.
- **Task support**: Helps with scheduling, reminders, and managing daily activities to promote independent living.

2. Common Applications

- **Screen reader enhancement**: Provides context and summaries to make digital content easier to navigate.
- **Captioning and transcription**: Generates real-time captions for meetings, lectures, and videos.
- **Accessible education**: Explains concepts in simpler terms or alternative formats to match a learner's needs.

- **Voice-controlled systems**: Integrates with smart assistants to execute tasks hands-free.

3. How It Works in Practice

1. **User interaction**: The individual communicates through text, speech, or assistive devices.
2. **Input processing**: ChatGPT-5 interprets the message and understands the user's intent.
3. **Content adaptation**: The model generates output in the most accessible format, such as text, speech, or simplified explanations.
4. **Integration with assistive technology**: Connects to tools like braille displays, text-to-speech systems, or visual recognition apps.
5. **Continuous personalization**: Learns the user's preferences over time to provide more tailored assistance.

4. Best Practices for Implementation

- Ensure privacy and security when handling sensitive user data.
- Collaborate with accessibility experts to design features that meet diverse needs.
- Allow customization so users can control the level of complexity and mode of communication.
- Test solutions with real users to ensure they work effectively in daily life.

Why This Matters

Accessibility is not just about compliance; it is about creating a more inclusive world where technology empowers everyone equally. ChatGPT-5 can be a key part of that effort, offering tools that help people with disabilities participate more fully in education, work, and social life.

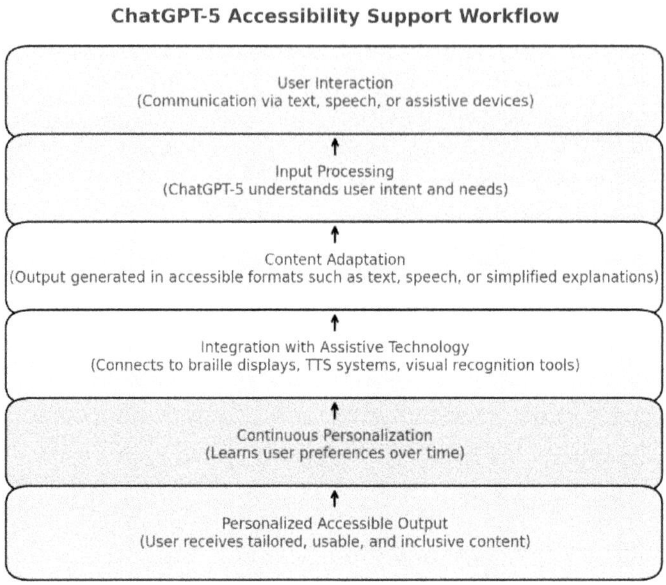

Multilingual Support

ChatGPT-5 offers robust multilingual capabilities, enabling seamless communication across a wide range of languages. This functionality helps bridge linguistic gaps in education, business, healthcare, and personal communication, allowing people from different cultural and language backgrounds to interact effectively. By understanding and generating text in multiple languages, ChatGPT-5 promotes inclusivity and access to information for users worldwide.

1. Benefits of Multilingual Support

- **Global accessibility**: Enables users to interact in their preferred language without requiring translation tools.
- **Cultural inclusivity**: Preserves context, idioms, and cultural nuances in communication.

- **Cross-border collaboration**: Facilitates international projects and partnerships.
- **Education enhancement**: Supports multilingual learning materials and tutoring.

2. Common Applications

- **Customer service**: Provides real-time support in multiple languages for global clients.
- **Healthcare communication**: Assists in translating medical information between providers and patients.
- **Education and training**: Delivers lessons, exercises, and feedback in the learner's chosen language.
- **Global research collaboration**: Summarizes and translates research findings for international teams.

3. How It Works in Practice

1. **Language detection**: ChatGPT-5 identifies the language of the input text automatically.
2. **Contextual understanding**: Interprets the meaning while preserving tone and cultural nuances.
3. **Response generation**: Produces output in the same language or translates it into the target language as requested.
4. **Quality review**: User verifies the accuracy and adjusts for specific terminology or regional preferences.
5. **Continuous learning**: Over time, ChatGPT-5 adapts to preferred vocabulary and phrasing styles for more personalized communication.

4. Best Practices for Implementation

- Specify the desired language in prompts for precise results.
- Provide context when translating technical or specialized material.
- Verify translations for critical communications to ensure accuracy.
- Encourage bilingual or multilingual review when working in high-stakes contexts.

Why This Matters

Language differences can create significant barriers to participation and understanding. By offering multilingual support, ChatGPT-5 reduces these barriers, making communication more equitable and accessible for individuals and organizations around the world.

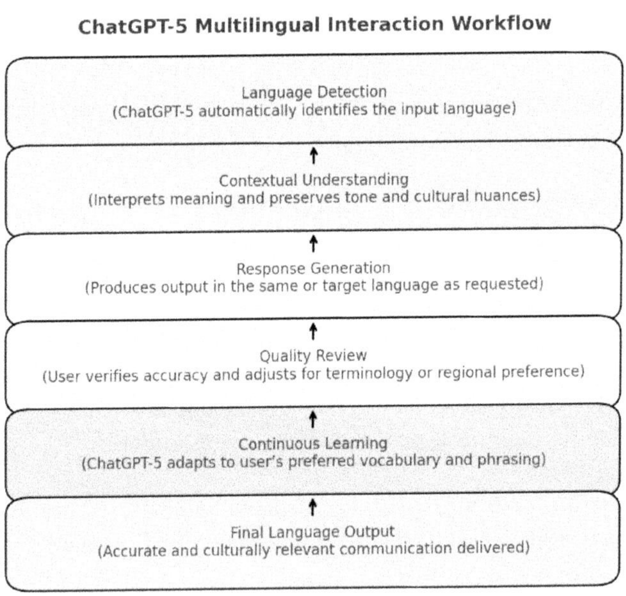

Bridging Digital Literacy Gaps

Digital literacy is essential for fully participating in modern society, yet many individuals lack the skills needed to navigate technology confidently. ChatGPT-5 can help bridge this gap by serving as a patient, adaptive, and accessible guide for users with varying levels of digital proficiency. Whether the challenge is understanding basic computer functions or learning to use complex online tools, ChatGPT-5 can provide step-by-step support in a clear and approachable way.

1. Benefits of ChatGPT-5 in Bridging Digital Literacy Gaps

- **Accessible guidance**: Offers simple, jargon-free explanations tailored to the user's understanding.
- **Interactive learning**: Provides real-time answers and clarification during tasks.
- **Skill progression**: Adapts lesson complexity as the user becomes more proficient.
- **Confidence building**: Encourages self-reliance through supportive instruction.

2. Common Applications

- **Basic computer skills**: Explains how to use email, word processors, or file storage.
- **Online safety**: Teaches how to recognize scams, protect passwords, and manage privacy settings.
- **Software training**: Guides users through installing, configuring, and operating applications.
- **Internet navigation**: Helps with using search engines, accessing online services, and participating in social media.

3. How It Works in Practice

1. **User inquiry**: The individual asks for help with a specific digital task.
2. **Skill assessment**: ChatGPT-5 gauges the user's current proficiency based on their questions and responses.
3. **Instructional guidance**: Provides step-by-step instructions in plain language, with optional images or diagrams.
4. **Real-time assistance**: Offers troubleshooting and additional explanations as the user works through the task.
5. **Skill reinforcement**: Suggests follow-up exercises to strengthen newly learned abilities.

4. Best Practices for Implementation

- Start with the simplest possible explanation before introducing advanced concepts.
- Use clear examples and analogies relevant to the user's experiences.
- Encourage users to try tasks independently with ChatGPT-5 as a safety net.
- Adapt instructions to different learning speeds and styles.

Why This Matters
Without digital literacy, individuals can be excluded from educational opportunities, employment prospects, and access to essential services. ChatGPT-5 can empower users to gain the skills they need, helping to close the digital divide and promote greater participation in the connected world.

ChatGPT-5 Digital Literacy Support Workflow

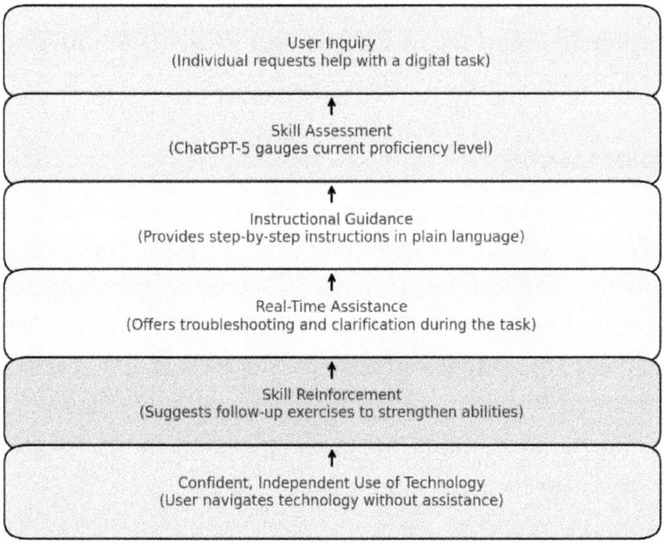

Part IV: Challenges, Risks, and Future Directions

Chapter 15 – Common Pitfalls and How to Avoid Them

Misinterpretations

Misinterpretations occur when ChatGPT-5 understands a prompt differently from what the user intended, leading to outputs that are inaccurate, irrelevant, or misleading. These misunderstandings can result from ambiguous wording, lack of context, cultural differences, or overly complex sentence structures. Since ChatGPT-5 relies on patterns learned from data rather than personal understanding, it can sometimes generate content that seems plausible but is not aligned with the user's goals.

1. Causes of Misinterpretations

- **Ambiguous language**: Vague or unclear terms make it difficult for the model to determine the correct meaning.
- **Insufficient context**: Without enough background, ChatGPT-5 may guess the intended meaning incorrectly.
- **Complex or nested questions**: Overly complicated queries increase the likelihood of confusion.
- **Cultural or linguistic differences**: Certain phrases or idioms may be understood differently across languages or regions.

2. Consequences of Misinterpretations

- **Incorrect information**: The output may contain factual inaccuracies or irrelevant details.
- **Wasted time**: Users may need to reformulate questions or verify answers repeatedly.

- **Reduced trust**: Frequent misunderstandings can make users hesitant to rely on the system.
- **Decision-making errors**: Misinterpretations in critical areas, such as healthcare or finance, can have serious consequences.

3. How to Avoid Misinterpretations

1. **Be clear and specific**: Use precise language and avoid vague terms.
2. **Provide context**: Include relevant background information or examples.
3. **Break down complex queries**: Ask multiple smaller questions instead of one large, complicated one.
4. **Clarify cultural references**: Explain idioms, metaphors, or context-specific terms.
5. **Review and iterate**: If the output seems off, rephrase the prompt and try again.

4. Example

- **Ineffective prompt**: "Tell me about the bank."
- **Effective prompt**: "Tell me about the role of commercial banks in the U.S. economy."

Why This Matters

Misinterpretations reduce efficiency and can lead to flawed outcomes if unchecked. By understanding the causes and taking steps to reduce them, users can significantly improve the accuracy and relevance of ChatGPT-5's responses, leading to more productive and reliable interactions.

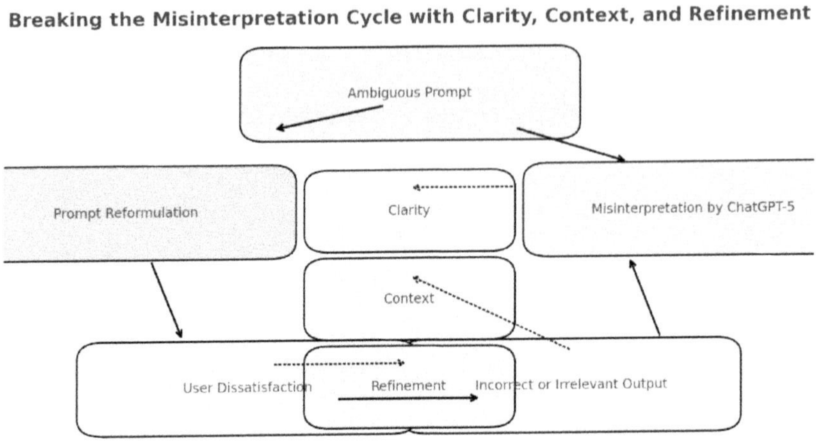

Over-reliance on AI

While ChatGPT-5 is an advanced and capable system, relying on it excessively can create vulnerabilities for individuals, businesses, and institutions. Over-reliance occurs when users treat AI-generated outputs as infallible or stop developing their own problem-solving, research, and decision-making skills. This dependence can reduce human oversight, diminish creativity, and increase the risk of accepting inaccurate or biased information without critical review.

1. Causes of Over-reliance

- **Convenience**: AI can deliver fast, detailed answers, making it tempting to use it as the sole source of information.
- **Perceived authority**: Well-structured responses may appear more credible than they actually are.
- **Skill erosion**: Users may avoid independent research or analysis over time.

- **Automation comfort**: Integrating AI into workflows can make manual verification seem unnecessary.

2. Consequences of Over-reliance

- **Inaccurate decisions**: Unverified AI outputs can lead to costly errors in business, legal, or medical contexts.
- **Reduced innovation**: Creativity may suffer when human brainstorming is replaced entirely by AI suggestions.
- **Ethical and legal risks**: Blind trust in AI can result in the misuse of sensitive or confidential information.
- **Loss of critical thinking**: Users may accept information without questioning its source or validity.

3. How to Avoid Over-reliance

1. **Verify information**: Cross-check AI outputs with credible human and institutional sources.
2. **Maintain human oversight**: Keep subject matter experts involved in decision-making processes.
3. **Use AI as a supplement**: Treat ChatGPT-5 as an assistant rather than a replacement for human judgment.
4. **Preserve core skills**: Continue practicing research, analysis, and creative thinking without AI assistance.
5. **Encourage balanced workflows**: Combine AI efficiency with human expertise for optimal results.

4. Example

- **Risk scenario**: A company fully automates its market research process using ChatGPT-5 and implements the recommendations without fact-checking, leading to poor investment choices.

- **Better approach**: Use ChatGPT-5 for initial data gathering and analysis, then have a research team validate and refine the findings before making decisions.

Why This Matters
AI is a powerful tool, but it is not infallible. By understanding the dangers of over-reliance and implementing safeguards, users can leverage ChatGPT-5 effectively while ensuring that human intelligence, oversight, and ethics remain central to decision-making.

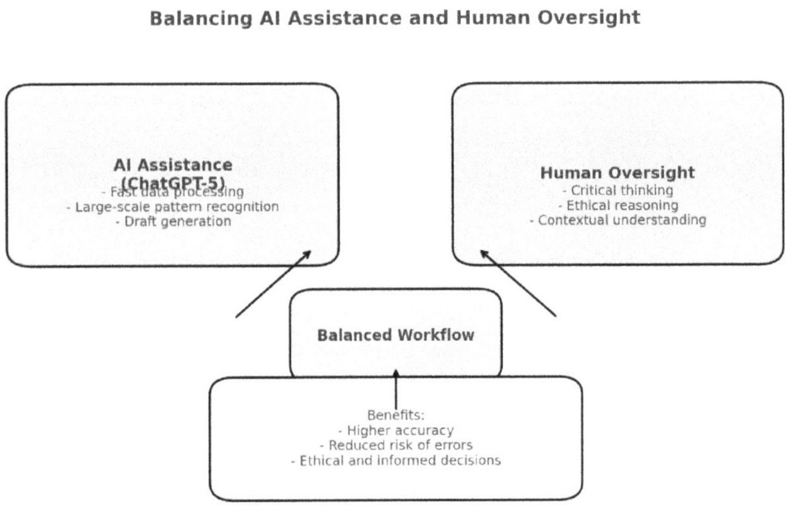

Hallucinations and Fact-checking

One of the most significant challenges when working with ChatGPT-5 is the risk of hallucinations. In the context of artificial intelligence, hallucinations occur when the system generates statements, facts, or references that appear convincing but are incorrect, misleading, or entirely fabricated. These outputs can result from limitations in training data, statistical predictions made without complete information, or an overconfident extrapolation of patterns that seem relevant but are not factual.

1. Causes of Hallucinations

- **Gaps in training data**: If certain information is missing or outdated, the model may attempt to fill in the blanks with plausible but false content.
- **Overgeneralization**: The system may apply patterns from one domain to another without valid reasoning.
- **Prompt ambiguity**: Vague or imprecise prompts can cause the model to make inaccurate assumptions.
- **Overconfidence in predictions**: The model is designed to produce coherent text, which can lead to confidently stated but incorrect facts.

2. Consequences of Hallucinations

- **Spread of misinformation**: Incorrect outputs can be repeated and shared, amplifying errors.
- **Loss of credibility**: Frequent inaccuracies reduce trust in both the AI and its users.
- **Potential harm in sensitive areas**: Inaccuracies in healthcare, legal, or financial contexts can have serious consequences.
- **Time wasted on corrections**: Users must spend additional effort verifying and fixing errors.

3. How to Avoid Hallucinations

1. **Fact-check systematically**: Always verify claims against authoritative sources before using or sharing them.

2. **Use domain experts**: In specialized fields, have subject matter experts review AI-generated content.
3. **Request sources**: Ask the AI to provide citations or indicate uncertainty if it is unsure.
4. **Break down queries**: Use multiple, specific prompts to reduce ambiguity and improve accuracy.
5. **Maintain skepticism**: Treat every AI output as a draft, not a final answer.

4. Example

- **Risk scenario**: A student asks ChatGPT-5 for the discovery date of a scientific phenomenon, and the AI confidently gives a plausible but incorrect year.
- **Better approach**: The student uses the AI's response as a lead, then confirms the date in peer-reviewed literature or a trusted database.

Why This Matters

Hallucinations undermine the reliability of AI-assisted work if left unchecked. Fact-checking is not just a safeguard but an essential step in using ChatGPT-5 responsibly. By making verification a standard part of the workflow, users can ensure that the speed and convenience of AI are matched by accuracy and trustworthiness.

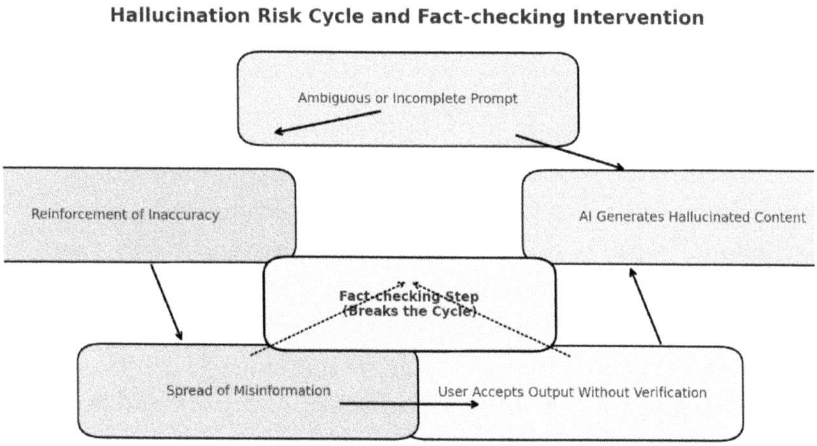
Hallucination Risk Cycle and Fact-checking Intervention
Ambiguous or Incomplete Prompt
Reinforcement of Inaccuracy
AI Generates Hallucinated Content
Fact-checking Step
(Breaks the Cycle)
Spread of Misinformation
User Accepts Output Without Verification

Chapter 16 – AI and Intellectual Property

Copyright Concerns

The rapid growth of AI systems like ChatGPT-5 has brought copyright concerns to the forefront of technological and legal discussions. While AI can generate text, images, music, and other creative works, questions remain about ownership, originality, and the legal boundaries of content creation when machine learning models are involved. These concerns are not only relevant for professional creators but also for businesses, educators, and everyday users who work with AI-generated materials.

1. Sources of Copyright Issues

- **Training data use**: AI models are trained on massive datasets that may include copyrighted materials. Even if the content is not directly copied, elements of style, structure, or wording may resemble protected works.
- **Output similarity**: AI-generated outputs may unintentionally reproduce copyrighted content, especially when prompts are highly specific or relate to well-known works.
- **Ambiguity of ownership**: Legal systems in many countries are still debating whether AI-generated works can be copyrighted, and if so, who holds the rights — the user, the developer, or neither.
- **Derivative works**: If AI-generated content is based on copyrighted input, it may be considered a derivative work that still falls under existing copyright protections.

2. Consequences of Ignoring Copyright Concerns

- **Legal disputes**: Using AI-generated content without checking for infringement risks lawsuits or takedown orders.

- **Reputational damage**: Organizations that misuse copyrighted material may face public criticism and loss of trust.
- **Financial penalties**: Copyright violations can lead to significant fines and settlement costs.
- **Restricted use of outputs**: Some platforms or publishers may reject AI-generated work that lacks clear copyright clearance.

3. How to Avoid Copyright Infringement

1. **Use original prompts**: Avoid prompts that mimic specific works too closely.
2. **Check outputs for similarity**: Use plagiarism detection tools to ensure originality.
3. **Rely on public domain and licensed sources**: When possible, limit AI training or prompts to material that is freely and legally usable.
4. **Understand platform policies**: Many AI tools, including ChatGPT-5, have terms of use that address copyright responsibility.
5. **When in doubt, seek legal advice**: For commercial projects, consult with intellectual property experts before publishing or distributing AI-generated content.

4. Example

- **Risk scenario**: A marketing agency uses ChatGPT-5 to write a slogan for a product, only to find that the wording closely matches a protected tagline from another brand.

- **Better approach**: The agency runs a trademark and copyright search before finalizing the slogan to ensure it is both original and legally safe.

Why This Matters

Copyright law protects the creative efforts of individuals and organizations, and its boundaries are being tested by the rise of AI. By being proactive and informed, users of ChatGPT-5 can enjoy the creative potential of the technology while respecting intellectual property rights.

Copyright Risk Pathway and Safe-use Checks

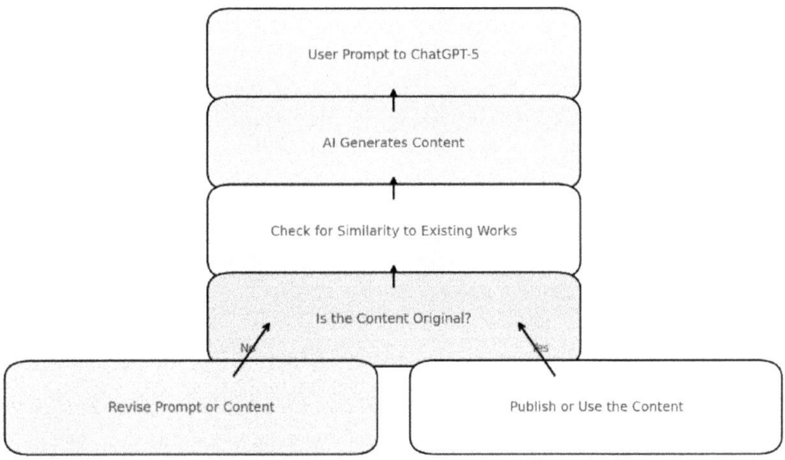

Plagiarism Checks

The integration of AI systems like ChatGPT-5 into writing, research, and creative processes has increased the importance of plagiarism detection. While ChatGPT-5 can produce original and diverse outputs, there remains the possibility that it may inadvertently generate material that is too similar to existing works. This can happen due to similarities in phrasing, structure, or factual presentation, especially if the prompt closely resembles existing content or if the generated text draws from common knowledge that is widely published.

1. Why Plagiarism Checks Are Important

- **Academic integrity**: Schools and universities require students to submit original work, making plagiarism detection essential in any AI-assisted writing.
- **Professional reputation**: Businesses, journalists, and authors can face reputational damage if accused of copying content.
- **Legal implications**: Copyright laws protect original works, and plagiarism can lead to legal disputes, even when it is unintentional.
- **Quality assurance**: A plagiarism check ensures that generated content is not only unique but also credible and trustworthy.

2. Causes of AI-Related Plagiarism Risks

- **Prompt similarity to known sources**: If the input prompt matches text from well-known books, articles, or online content, the AI might produce a similar version.
- **Common phrasing in niche topics**: In specialized fields, there are limited ways to express certain facts, which can lead to unintentional similarity.
- **Unverified paraphrasing**: ChatGPT-5 might rephrase existing content without enough changes to be considered original.

3. Best Practices for Conducting Plagiarism Checks

1. **Use professional plagiarism detection tools**: Platforms like Turnitin, Grammarly, and Copyscape can help identify similarities with published material.
2. **Cross-check multiple sections**: Instead of checking only final drafts, verify originality at key stages of writing.
3. **Revise flagged content**: If similarities are found, rephrase ideas in your own words and add new perspectives or supporting details.
4. **Cite sources correctly**: When drawing from known works, ensure proper attribution to avoid claims of plagiarism.
5. **Combine human review with AI**: Use both automated plagiarism detection and human editorial oversight for the most reliable results.

4. Example

- **Risk scenario**: A student uses ChatGPT-5 to write a research paper. After submission, the professor's plagiarism checker flags 30% similarity with an online journal article.
- **Better approach**: The student runs the draft through a plagiarism detection tool before submission, identifies the matching sections, and rewrites them to ensure originality.

Why This Matters

Plagiarism checks are not only a safeguard against accusations of academic dishonesty or copyright violation, they are also a step toward building trust in AI-assisted work. With proactive verification, users can ensure that the output from ChatGPT-5 reflects their own ideas and meets the ethical and legal standards of their field.

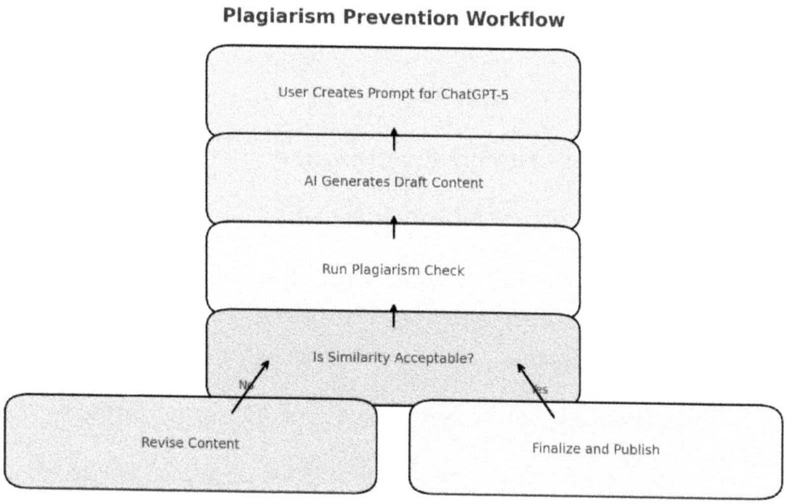

Attribution Best Practices

When using ChatGPT-5 for writing, research, creative projects, or technical tasks, proper attribution is essential to maintain transparency, respect intellectual property rights, and build trust with audiences. While AI can generate original ideas and content, it is important to clearly identify when its output has been used, particularly in academic, professional, or public-facing contexts.

1. Why Attribution Matters

- **Transparency**: Letting readers or stakeholders know when AI assistance has been used ensures honesty and credibility.
- **Ethical compliance**: Some institutions and publishers have explicit policies requiring disclosure of AI involvement.
- **Legal considerations**: Proper attribution helps avoid disputes over originality or authorship.

- **Collaboration acknowledgment**: AI is a tool that supports human creativity and problem-solving, and acknowledging its role reflects fair credit distribution.

2. Core Principles of Effective Attribution

1. **Be specific about AI involvement**
   - Clearly state when ChatGPT-5 contributed to the work, specifying whether it was used for idea generation, drafting, or refining.
2. **Differentiate between human and AI contributions**
   - Mark AI-generated sections or ideas and ensure that your own input is clearly visible and substantial.
3. **Cite sources for factual content**
   - Even when AI provides facts, verify them and reference credible sources. Attribution to the AI does not replace the need for proper citations.
4. **Follow organizational or industry guidelines**
   - Align your attribution practices with the policies of your workplace, academic institution, or publishing body.
5. **Maintain consistency**
   - Use the same style and placement for AI attribution throughout your document or project.

3. Examples of AI Attribution

- **Academic paper**:
  "Portions of the literature review were drafted with the assistance of ChatGPT-5 and were subsequently edited for accuracy and clarity by the author."

- **Business report**:
  "AI assistance from ChatGPT-5 was used to summarize market trends. All interpretations and conclusions are the responsibility of the author."

- **Creative writing**:
  "Story concept and outline were developed collaboratively with ChatGPT-5, with all narrative refinements provided by the author."

4. Mistakes to Avoid in Attribution

- Omitting AI acknowledgment entirely when substantial portions were generated or heavily influenced by it.
- Using vague statements such as *"AI helped with this"* without clarifying how.
- Presenting AI-generated work as fully original human output in contexts where disclosure is required.

Why This Matters
Following attribution best practices not only fulfills ethical and legal obligations but also positions AI as a respected tool in collaborative creation. Proper acknowledgment fosters transparency, builds trust, and ensures that both the human and machine contributions are recognized appropriately.

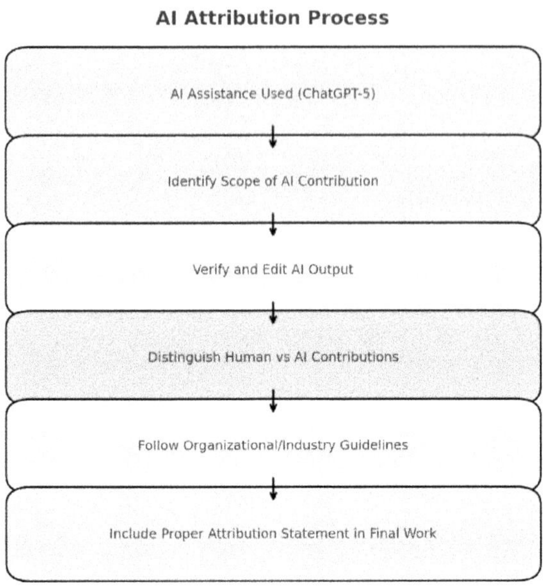
AI Attribution Process
AI Assistance Used (ChatGPT-5)
Identify Scope of AI Contribution
Verify and Edit AI Output
Distinguish Human vs AI Contributions
Follow Organizational/Industry Guidelines
Include Proper Attribution Statement in Final Work

Chapter 17 – The Future of Conversational AI

Trends Beyond GPT-5

While GPT-5 represents a significant milestone in the evolution of conversational AI, it is not the endpoint. The trajectory of AI development suggests that future systems will be more capable, contextually aware, and integrated into human life. Observing current research, industry movements, and technological progress, several trends emerge that point to what lies beyond GPT-5.

1. Greater Contextual Awareness and Memory
Models after GPT-5 are expected to handle much longer context windows, retaining details from earlier interactions across days or even weeks. This persistent memory could enable more personalized and coherent conversations that evolve naturally over time. It would allow AI to follow up on past discussions, remember user preferences, and adapt responses to long-term goals.

2. Improved Multimodal Integration
Although GPT-5 already processes text, images, and audio, the next generations may seamlessly integrate additional input types such as video, real-time sensor data, and virtual environment interactions. This expansion will make AI more versatile in fields like telemedicine, real-time translation, and immersive entertainment.

3. More Accurate and Reliable Outputs
One of the main criticisms of large language models is their tendency to produce hallucinations. Future systems will likely integrate real-time fact-checking, knowledge verification layers, and dynamic database connections to improve reliability and accuracy. This will make them more trustworthy for decision-making in high-stakes fields like law, medicine, and engineering.

4. Enhanced Personalization
AI models will increasingly tailor their behavior, tone, and responses

to each user's communication style, cultural background, and expertise level. Such personalization could extend to building individualized knowledge profiles that help the AI better anticipate user needs.

5. Ethical and Legal Integration
The next generation of conversational AI will likely include built-in compliance systems that adhere to laws, industry standards, and ethical guidelines in real time. This could involve automated plagiarism detection, copyright compliance, and fairness checks before content is delivered to the user.

6. Collaboration with Other AI Systems
Instead of functioning as standalone models, future conversational AIs may operate as part of multi-agent ecosystems, working alongside specialized AI tools for reasoning, simulation, or creativity. This would make AI assistants more like intelligent collaborators capable of orchestrating complex workflows.

7. Movement Toward Artificial General Intelligence (AGI)
Although true AGI remains a long-term aspiration, the increasing depth of reasoning, contextual awareness, and adaptability in AI models suggests a gradual movement toward systems that can understand and perform a much broader range of human-like cognitive tasks.

Why This Matters
Understanding trends beyond GPT-5 prepares individuals and organizations for the rapid changes that will shape how we communicate, learn, and work with AI. These advancements will bring both opportunities for innovation and challenges that demand careful planning, regulation, and responsible use.

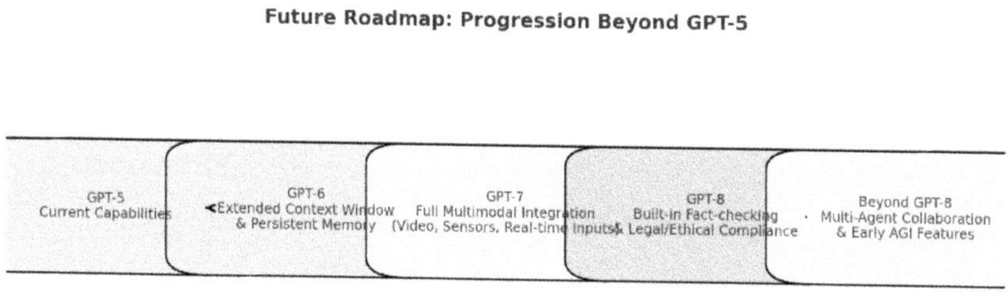

AI-Human Collaboration

As AI technology advances beyond GPT-5, the relationship between humans and AI is evolving from simple tool use to deeper forms of collaboration. AI-human collaboration is not just about replacing human effort with automation; it is about combining the unique strengths of each to achieve outcomes that neither could accomplish alone. This partnership is expected to redefine how we work, create, and solve problems in the coming years.

1. Complementary Strengths

Humans bring creativity, emotional intelligence, ethical judgment, and cultural context to the table. AI contributes speed, scalability, vast information recall, and advanced analytical capabilities. By combining these strengths, teams can achieve both precision and innovation at unprecedented levels.

2. Real-time Co-creation

With improved context awareness, AI models are becoming more effective as real-time collaborators. Writers can brainstorm plot points with AI while coders can debug in partnership with the model. Designers can merge human vision with AI-generated variations to reach creative solutions more efficiently.

3. Decision-making Support
In business, healthcare, and research, AI can process vast datasets, highlight patterns, and suggest evidence-based options while leaving the final decision to human judgment. This shared approach ensures that decisions benefit from both computational rigor and human values.

4. Education and Skills Augmentation
AI-human collaboration in education can create personalized learning experiences, with AI providing adaptive exercises and humans offering mentorship and guidance. In the workplace, AI can handle repetitive or data-heavy tasks, allowing humans to focus on strategic thinking and innovation.

5. Collaboration Across Disciplines
Future conversational AI may act as a bridge between disciplines by translating jargon, identifying shared goals, and proposing solutions that integrate knowledge from multiple fields. This could accelerate interdisciplinary research and innovation.

6. Ethical Safeguards in Collaboration
As AI becomes a partner in decision-making, it is critical to establish clear ethical boundaries. Humans must retain final authority, especially in situations involving moral judgment, legal compliance, or human well-being.

Why This Matters
The future of AI-human collaboration will shape how knowledge is created, shared, and applied. If designed and managed responsibly, this relationship can magnify human potential while ensuring that AI serves human interests rather than replacing them.

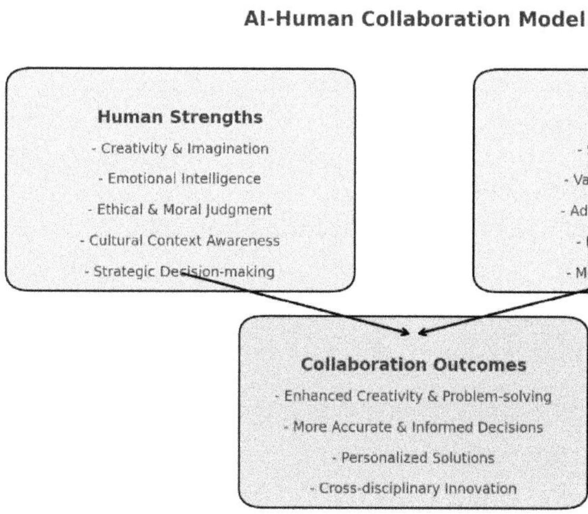

Predictions for GPT-6 and Beyond

The development of GPT-6 and later generations will likely represent a shift from rapid capability expansion toward more refined, reliable, and contextually aware systems. While GPT-5 already delivers significant advances in reasoning, multimodal integration, and context handling, its successors are expected to push the boundaries of both performance and application diversity. Several predictions can be made based on current research and industry direction.

1. Dramatically Expanded Context Windows
GPT-6 may be able to process and recall information across extremely long conversations or documents, possibly spanning entire books, technical manuals, or multi-day interactions. This would allow users to work on complex projects with an AI partner without losing continuity or having to restate prior details.

2. Native Multimodal Mastery
While GPT-5 can handle text, images, and audio, GPT-6 and beyond

may integrate video understanding, spatial reasoning, and real-time sensor data. Such capabilities could open new possibilities in medical imaging diagnostics, autonomous system monitoring, and fully immersive AI-driven simulations.

3. Embedded Real-time Verification
Future models may include built-in verification layers that continuously cross-check outputs against trusted databases, scholarly literature, and real-time information feeds. This will greatly reduce the risk of inaccuracies and make the AI safer for high-stakes decision-making.

4. Deep Personalization Engines
Advanced personalization could allow GPT-6 to learn and adapt to individual user goals, communication style, and domain expertise. This would enable more tailored responses, better learning support, and context-specific recommendations without compromising privacy.

5. Increased Interoperability with Other AI Agents
The trend toward multi-agent systems suggests that GPT-6 may be able to coordinate tasks with other specialized AI tools in real time. For example, it could collaborate with a data analysis agent, a design generation system, and a knowledge retrieval engine in a single conversation.

6. Adaptive Ethical Reasoning
With stricter regulations on AI use emerging globally, GPT-6 may incorporate dynamic ethical reasoning protocols that adjust to the legal and cultural context of the user. This would ensure compliance with local rules while maintaining fairness and inclusivity.

7. Movement Toward AGI Milestones
While true AGI may still be years away, GPT-6 and later models will likely display increasingly generalized reasoning skills, more human-like understanding of intent, and improved ability to transfer

knowledge across very different tasks. These advancements could bring AI closer to functioning as a truly universal assistant.

Why This Matters

Anticipating the capabilities of GPT-6 and beyond helps individuals, organizations, and policymakers prepare for the opportunities and challenges that come with more powerful conversational AI. Responsible development, transparency, and collaboration between humans and AI will be critical in ensuring that these advancements benefit society as a whole.

Predicted Evolution of GPT Models: GPT-5 to GPT-8 and Beyond

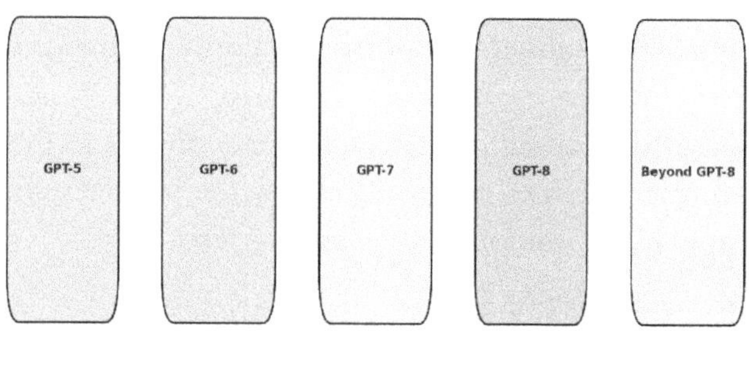

Part V: Mastery Through Practice

Chapter 18 – Prompt Playgrounds

Exercises

A prompt playground is a space where users can experiment with ChatGPT-5 in an open-ended and low-pressure environment. It allows learners to try different styles of prompts, observe the outputs, and refine their approach to improve results. To truly master ChatGPT-5, practice must be varied and should target three key domains: creativity, logic, and problem-solving.

1. Creativity Exercises

These exercises help expand your imagination and explore unconventional ideas. Examples include:

- Asking ChatGPT-5 to invent a new fictional world with unique rules, geography, and culture.
- Requesting an unusual twist on a well-known story, such as telling Cinderella from the point of view of the glass slipper.
- Generating marketing slogans for a product that does not yet exist.
  Creativity-focused prompts encourage the AI to think beyond common patterns, which also helps the user learn how to shape unconventional but engaging responses.

2. Logic Exercises

Logic-based prompts focus on structured reasoning and consistency. Examples include:

- Designing a puzzle or riddle and asking ChatGPT-5 to solve it step by step.

- Testing the AI's reasoning by giving it a set of facts and asking it to determine what is true or false.
- Presenting a scenario with multiple variables and asking it to find the optimal outcome.
  These exercises sharpen the AI's analytical capabilities while helping the user learn to guide the model toward precision and coherence.

3. Problem-solving Exercises
Problem-solving prompts are aimed at practical applications. Examples include:

- Asking ChatGPT-5 to help troubleshoot a software error with specific details of the situation.
- Presenting a real-world challenge, such as designing a cost-effective event plan with certain constraints.
- Requesting step-by-step instructions for completing a technical task, such as setting up a secure network.
  This type of practice builds skill in directing the AI toward useful, actionable, and context-aware outputs.

Why It Matters
By engaging in a balanced mix of creativity, logic, and problem-solving exercises, users develop a deeper understanding of ChatGPT-5's capabilities and limitations. The playground becomes more than a testing space; it turns into a training arena where both user skill and AI responsiveness improve together.

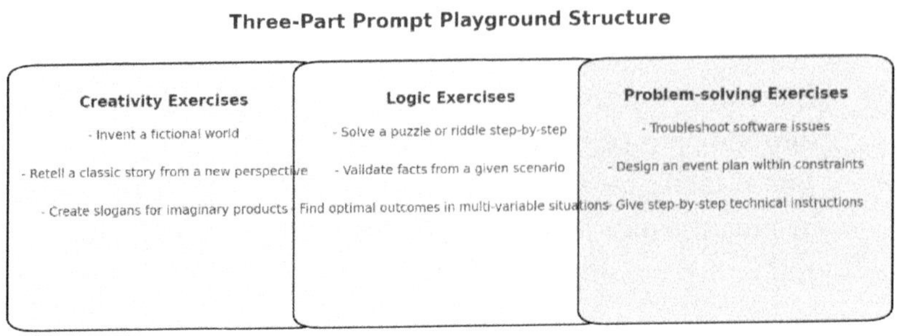

Timed Challenge Prompts

Timed challenge prompts are a practical and engaging way to improve both user skill and AI responsiveness. The core idea is to set a specific time limit for ChatGPT-5 to produce an answer, which simulates real-world conditions where quick, accurate responses are essential. These challenges push the user to think strategically about prompt construction and help the AI adapt to delivering concise, relevant, and fast results.

1. Purpose of Timed Challenges

Timed challenges are designed to test three aspects of AI interaction: clarity of the initial prompt, speed of response, and quality under time pressure. In many professional and academic environments, quick turnaround times are critical, so practicing within set limits builds readiness for real scenarios.

2. Examples of Timed Challenges

- **Creative Timed Writing**: Ask ChatGPT-5 to write a 100-word short story in 60 seconds based on a given theme or character.

- **Logic and Problem-solving Speed Test**: Provide a mathematical puzzle or logic problem with a short time window to solve it.
- **Rapid Research**: Request a quick summary of a topic in under 90 seconds, with a strict word count limit.

3. Benefits for Users
Timed prompts force users to be deliberate in how they phrase requests. Since there is no room for wasted words or vague instructions, users learn to eliminate ambiguity. This improves the overall skill of crafting clear, focused prompts even when no time pressure is involved.

4. Benefits for AI Interaction
For the AI, time-limited tasks promote efficient content generation. While ChatGPT-5 cannot "feel" urgency, designing prompts with time constraints often encourages the model to prioritize clarity and brevity over unnecessary elaboration.

5. Combining Timed Challenges with Feedback Loops
After each timed session, reviewing the output to identify strengths and weaknesses can lead to targeted improvement. For example, if the AI misses key details, the prompt can be adjusted for better precision in future attempts.

Why This Matters
Timed challenge prompts are not only a fun way to engage with ChatGPT-5, they are also a skill-building exercise that blends creativity, problem-solving, and clear communication. This makes them an ideal addition to any structured practice routine within a prompt playground.

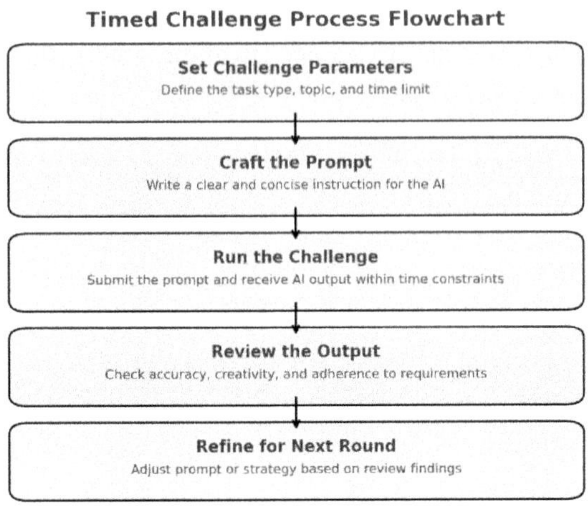

Reverse-engineering Prompts

Reverse-engineering prompts is a method where the user examines an AI-generated output and works backward to determine the original or likely prompt that produced it. This technique builds a deeper understanding of how ChatGPT-5 interprets instructions, which in turn helps the user become more precise and effective in their prompt crafting.

1. Purpose of Reverse-engineering

The main goal of this practice is to learn the relationship between the wording of a prompt and the resulting output. By identifying which instructions could have led to a given answer, users gain insight into the model's decision-making and language patterns.

2. How It Works

- **Step 1: Select an Output** – Choose a piece of AI-generated text, whether it is a short answer, a creative story, or a technical explanation.

- **Step 2: Identify Key Clues** – Look for structure, tone, level of detail, and subject matter as hints for the type of prompt used.
- **Step 3: Recreate the Prompt** – Write a prompt that you believe would produce a similar result.
- **Step 4: Test and Compare** – Input your recreated prompt into ChatGPT-5 and compare the new output with the original.

3. Benefits of Reverse-engineering

- **Improves Prompt Accuracy** – Understanding how certain wording affects results allows for more targeted prompt design.
- **Enhances Creative Flexibility** – Users learn to reframe ideas in multiple ways to achieve different output styles.
- **Reveals AI Tendencies** – Patterns in AI responses become more noticeable, which can be used to avoid undesired styles or biases.

4. Advanced Practice Variations

- **Partial Reconstruction** – Try to guess only part of the prompt and see if the AI fills in the rest similarly.
- **Blind Testing** – Have someone else create the original prompt and see if you can recreate it without prior hints.
- **Style Matching** – Attempt to replicate an output's tone and structure even if the topic is different.

Why This Matters

Reverse-engineering prompts trains the user to think like the AI, anticipating how ChatGPT-5 might interpret given instructions. This strengthens both creative and technical control, making it easier to produce high-quality, targeted responses in any context.

Reverse-engineering Prompts

Reverse-engineering prompts is a method where the user examines an AI-generated output and works backward to determine the original or likely prompt that produced it. This technique builds a deeper understanding of how ChatGPT-5 interprets instructions, which in turn helps the user become more precise and effective in their prompt crafting.

1. Purpose of Reverse-engineering
The main goal of this practice is to learn the relationship between the wording of a prompt and the resulting output. By identifying which instructions could have led to a given answer, users gain insight into the model's decision-making and language patterns.

2. How It Works

- **Step 1: Select an Output** – Choose a piece of AI-generated text, whether it is a short answer, a creative story, or a technical explanation.
- **Step 2: Identify Key Clues** – Look for structure, tone, level of detail, and subject matter as hints for the type of prompt used.
- **Step 3: Recreate the Prompt** – Write a prompt that you believe would produce a similar result.
- **Step 4: Test and Compare** – Input your recreated prompt into ChatGPT-5 and compare the new output with the original.

3. Benefits of Reverse-engineering

- **Improves Prompt Accuracy** – Understanding how certain wording affects results allows for more targeted prompt design.
- **Enhances Creative Flexibility** – Users learn to reframe ideas in multiple ways to achieve different output styles.
- **Reveals AI Tendencies** – Patterns in AI responses become more noticeable, which can be used to avoid undesired styles or biases.

4. Advanced Practice Variations

- **Partial Reconstruction** – Try to guess only part of the prompt and see if the AI fills in the rest similarly.
- **Blind Testing** – Have someone else create the original prompt and see if you can recreate it without prior hints.
- **Style Matching** – Attempt to replicate an output's tone and structure even if the topic is different.

Why This Matters

Reverse-engineering prompts trains the user to think like the AI, anticipating how ChatGPT-5 might interpret given instructions. This strengthens both creative and technical control, making it easier to produce high-quality, targeted responses in any context.

Reverse-engineering Prompts: Step by Step

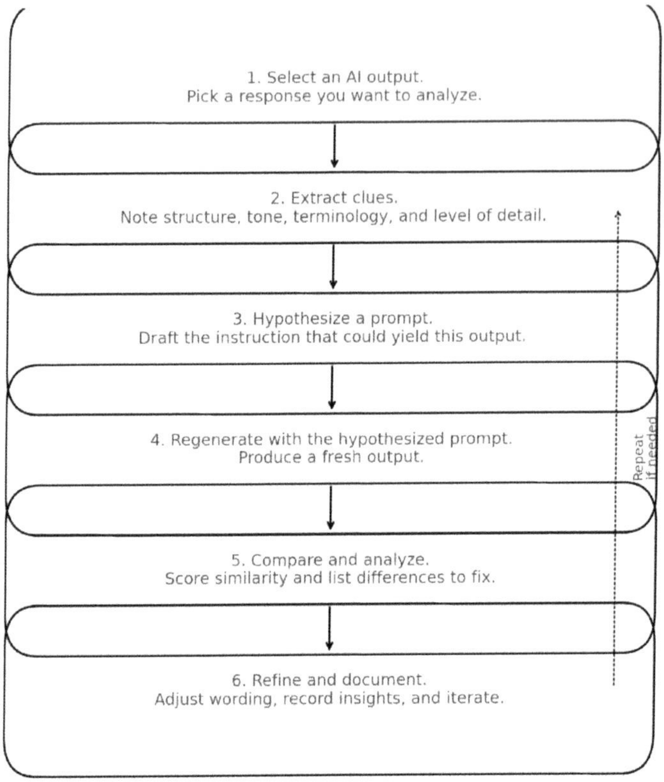

Chapter 19 – Real-World Case Studies

Business Transformation Examples

The adoption of ChatGPT-5 in business operations has led to significant transformations across multiple industries. These changes are not simply incremental improvements but rather shifts in how work is performed, how decisions are made, and how customers interact with companies.

1. Customer Engagement Revitalization
One retail company integrated ChatGPT-5 into its online store's customer service platform. Previously, customers faced long wait times for responses and inconsistent answers from human agents. By training ChatGPT-5 on the company's product catalogs, FAQs, and brand guidelines, the business was able to provide instant, consistent, and accurate responses to customer inquiries. This not only improved satisfaction scores but also increased conversion rates because potential buyers received the information they needed without delay.

2. Content Operations Overhaul
A global marketing agency adopted ChatGPT-5 to generate initial drafts of blog posts, social media captions, and product descriptions. Human editors then refined the AI-generated drafts for style, tone, and accuracy. This approach reduced production time by over 50 percent, freeing up creative teams to focus on higher-level campaign strategies. The integration also allowed the agency to rapidly test different content variations, improving campaign performance based on real-time engagement data.

3. Data-Driven Decision Making
A mid-sized logistics company used ChatGPT-5 to process and summarize vast amounts of shipment, fuel consumption, and route optimization data. Instead of waiting for periodic analyst reports, decision-makers could query the AI for instant insights. For example, managers could ask which routes had the highest delays last quarter

and receive a concise analysis with recommendations. This ability to act on near real-time data improved efficiency and reduced operational costs.

4. Knowledge Management Transformation
A healthcare organization employed ChatGPT-5 as an internal knowledge assistant for its staff. Medical personnel could query the AI for procedural guidelines, drug information, and policy documents without sifting through lengthy manuals. This quick access to reliable information reduced administrative burdens, allowing professionals to focus more on patient care.

5. Strategic Planning Enhancement
A financial services firm used ChatGPT-5 during strategic planning workshops. Executives could brainstorm potential scenarios and instantly get AI-generated summaries, market analysis, and possible risks. This accelerated the planning process and improved scenario evaluation by introducing diverse perspectives derived from massive training datasets.

Why This Matters
These examples highlight that business transformation with ChatGPT-5 is not about replacing humans but about augmenting their capabilities. By automating repetitive tasks, surfacing hidden insights, and enabling faster responses, companies can redirect their resources toward innovation and long-term value creation.

Education Success Stories

The integration of ChatGPT-5 into educational settings has led to meaningful improvements in how students learn, how teachers teach, and how institutions deliver knowledge. These success stories illustrate the diverse ways that AI can serve as both a teaching partner and a personalized learning resource.

1. Personalized Tutoring for Struggling Students
A public high school introduced ChatGPT-5 as a supplemental

tutoring tool for students in mathematics and science. Learners who were falling behind received tailored explanations, step-by-step problem-solving guides, and interactive quizzes that matched their current skill levels. Teachers reported that students using the AI tutor improved their grades by an average of 15 percent over one semester, with greater engagement in class discussions.

2. Language Learning Acceleration
An online language school integrated ChatGPT-5 into its platform to help students practice conversational skills in real time. The AI simulated various scenarios, from ordering food in a restaurant to attending a job interview, while also providing instant grammar and vocabulary feedback. Learners reported higher confidence and reduced anxiety when speaking with native speakers, leading to increased course completion rates.

3. Remote Learning Enhancement
A university with a large online student body used ChatGPT-5 to provide 24/7 academic assistance across different subjects. The AI could explain complex concepts, summarize lecture notes, and help students prepare for exams. This constant availability meant that students in different time zones or with unconventional schedules had equal access to high-quality academic support.

4. Special Needs Support
A middle school leveraged ChatGPT-5 to assist students with learning disabilities. For example, the AI could rephrase complex instructions into simpler language, provide alternative explanations using visual aids, and read text aloud for students with dyslexia. Teachers found that these adaptations allowed more inclusive participation in the classroom.

5. Research Skill Development
A group of graduate students in education research used ChatGPT-5 to refine their research questions, summarize literature, and generate preliminary outlines for their theses. This saved significant time in the

early stages of the research process, allowing them to focus more on data collection and analysis.

Why This Matters

These stories demonstrate that ChatGPT-5 does not replace educators but instead enhances their reach and effectiveness. By providing on-demand, adaptive, and interactive learning support, the AI empowers students to take greater control over their own education while freeing educators to focus on mentorship and higher-level teaching strategies.

Education Success Stories

The integration of ChatGPT-5 into educational settings has led to meaningful improvements in how students learn, how teachers teach, and how institutions deliver knowledge. These success stories illustrate the diverse ways that AI can serve as both a teaching partner and a personalized learning resource.

1. Personalized Tutoring for Struggling Students

A public high school introduced ChatGPT-5 as a supplemental tutoring tool for students in mathematics and science. Learners who were falling behind received tailored explanations, step-by-step problem-solving guides, and interactive quizzes that matched their current skill levels. Teachers reported that students using the AI tutor improved their grades by an average of 15 percent over one semester, with greater engagement in class discussions.

2. Language Learning Acceleration

An online language school integrated ChatGPT-5 into its platform to help students practice conversational skills in real time. The AI simulated various scenarios, from ordering food in a restaurant to attending a job interview, while also providing instant grammar and vocabulary feedback. Learners reported higher confidence and reduced anxiety when speaking with native speakers, leading to increased course completion rates.

3. Remote Learning Enhancement

A university with a large online student body used ChatGPT-5 to provide 24/7 academic assistance across different subjects. The AI could explain complex concepts, summarize lecture notes, and help students prepare for exams. This constant availability meant that students in different time zones or with unconventional schedules had equal access to high-quality academic support.

4. Special Needs Support

A middle school leveraged ChatGPT-5 to assist students with learning disabilities. For example, the AI could rephrase complex instructions into simpler language, provide alternative explanations using visual aids, and read text aloud for students with dyslexia. Teachers found that these adaptations allowed more inclusive participation in the classroom.

5. Research Skill Development

A group of graduate students in education research used ChatGPT-5 to refine their research questions, summarize literature, and generate preliminary outlines for their theses. This saved significant time in the early stages of the research process, allowing them to focus more on data collection and analysis.

Why This Matters

These stories demonstrate that ChatGPT-5 does not replace educators but instead enhances their reach and effectiveness. By providing on-demand, adaptive, and interactive learning support, the AI empowers students to take greater control over their own education while freeing educators to focus on mentorship and higher-level teaching strategies.

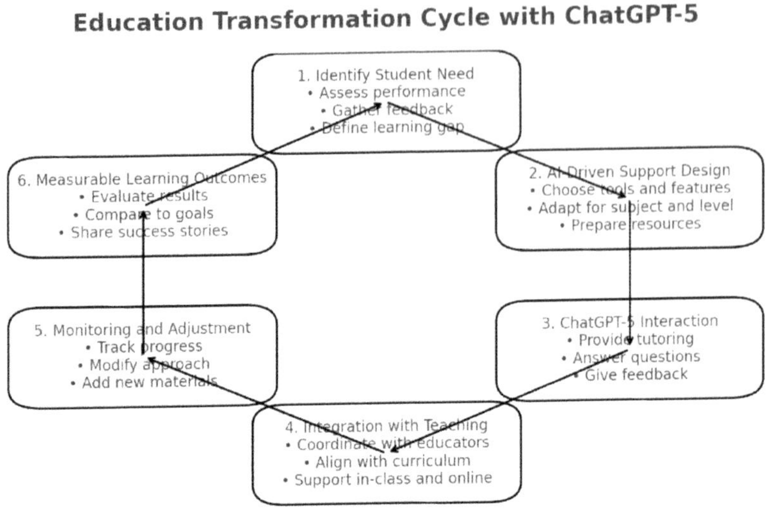

<u>Research Breakthroughs</u>

The introduction of ChatGPT-5 into research workflows has accelerated discovery and improved efficiency across multiple fields. Its ability to process vast quantities of information, generate hypotheses, and provide clear summaries has led to tangible breakthroughs for both individual researchers and collaborative teams.

1. Accelerating Literature Reviews

In biomedical research, a team faced delays in synthesizing findings from hundreds of journal articles. ChatGPT-5 was trained on their specific topic and used to summarize key points, highlight conflicting data, and point out gaps in current understanding. This reduced the review phase from months to weeks, allowing experiments to begin much sooner.

2. Enhancing Cross-Disciplinary Collaboration

A climate science project involved experts from meteorology, oceanography, and environmental policy. ChatGPT-5 acted as a communication bridge by translating highly technical language into accessible terms for all team members. This improved the clarity of interdisciplinary meetings and helped the team develop integrated models for climate prediction.

3. Hypothesis Generation at Scale
A genetics research lab leveraged ChatGPT-5 to analyze patterns in genomic data and suggest potential genetic markers for disease susceptibility. The AI proposed several hypotheses that human researchers had not previously considered. One of these hypotheses led to the discovery of a potential biomarker for early disease detection, which is now undergoing peer review.

4. Rapid Data Interpretation
In particle physics, vast experimental datasets can take months to interpret. ChatGPT-5 was paired with domain-specific analysis tools to quickly flag unusual patterns worth investigating. This accelerated the identification of anomalies that may represent new physical phenomena.

5. Democratizing Research for Under-Resourced Institutions
Small research institutes without access to large teams of analysts used ChatGPT-5 to conduct sophisticated literature analysis and data exploration. This enabled them to compete with better-funded organizations, bringing fresh perspectives and innovations into their fields.

Why This Matters
These examples demonstrate that ChatGPT-5 is not a replacement for human researchers but rather an amplifier of human intelligence. By handling time-consuming tasks like data scanning, cross-referencing, and hypothesis refinement, the AI allows scientists to devote more energy to creative and strategic elements of research. The result is faster progress and more opportunities for breakthrough discoveries.

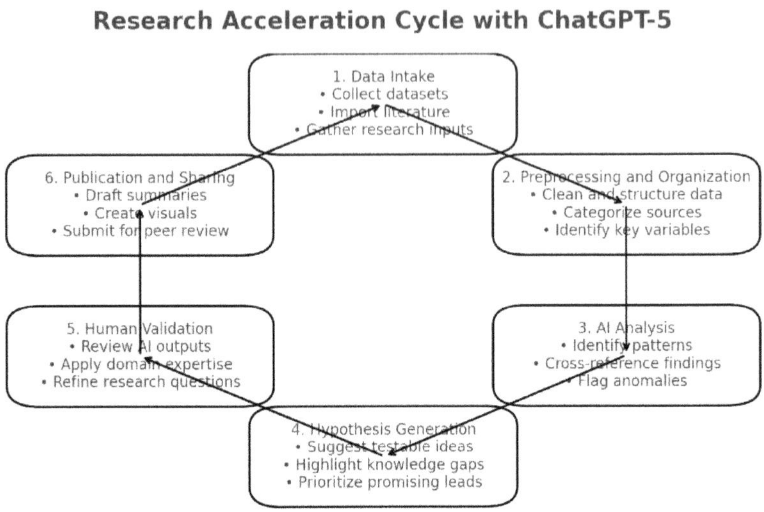
Research Acceleration Cycle with ChatGPT-5
1. Data Intake
• Collect datasets
• Import literature
• Gather research inputs
2. Preprocessing and Organization
• Clean and structure data
• Categorize sources
• Identify key variables
3. AI Analysis
• Identify patterns
• Cross-reference findings
• Flag anomalies
4. Hypothesis Generation
• Suggest testable ideas
• Highlight knowledge gaps
• Prioritize promising leads
5. Human Validation
• Review AI outputs
• Apply domain expertise
• Refine research questions
6. Publication and Sharing
• Draft summaries
• Create visuals
• Submit for peer review

Chapter 20 – Building Your AI Workflow

Choosing the Right Tools

Selecting the right tools is one of the most critical steps in building a productive AI workflow with ChatGPT-5. The tools you choose determine not only the efficiency of your work but also the accuracy, flexibility, and scalability of your AI-powered processes. While ChatGPT-5 is at the center of this ecosystem, its capabilities expand significantly when combined with complementary platforms, plugins, and integrations.

1. Define Your Objectives First

Before deciding on any tool, clarify your goals. Are you focusing on content creation, data analysis, customer service, education, or research? Each objective may require a different mix of features and integrations. For example, a marketing team might prioritize image generation plugins, while a data scientist may value API connectivity and advanced analytics integrations.

2. Evaluate Compatibility

Choose tools that integrate seamlessly with ChatGPT-5. This ensures smooth data flow and eliminates unnecessary manual work. Check whether the tool offers native connectors, API endpoints, or direct plugin support.

3. Consider User Experience

A tool that is powerful but difficult to use can slow down your workflow. Prioritize interfaces that are intuitive and allow quick access to the most frequently used features. If multiple team members will be involved, look for platforms with customizable permissions and collaboration features.

4. Focus on Data Security

Ensure that the tools you choose comply with relevant data protection regulations such as GDPR or CCPA. Look for encryption, access controls, and transparent privacy policies. This is especially important if you are handling sensitive or proprietary information.

5. Test Before Committing
Many tools offer free trials or limited free versions. Use these opportunities to experiment and see how the tool performs in real-world conditions. Pay attention to speed, accuracy, and how well it handles your specific tasks.

6. Plan for Scalability
Your needs may grow over time. Select tools that can handle increased workloads without requiring a complete change of systems. This includes checking for higher-tier plans, automation capabilities, and cloud-based scalability.

7. Balance Cost with Value
The most expensive tool is not always the best. Focus on the overall return on investment by considering the time saved, the quality of results, and the potential for workflow automation.

Why This Matters
A well-chosen set of tools can transform ChatGPT-5 from a standalone AI into the centerpiece of a highly efficient, integrated workflow. The right choices will help you streamline processes, reduce repetitive tasks, and unlock advanced capabilities that maximize the potential of AI in your work.

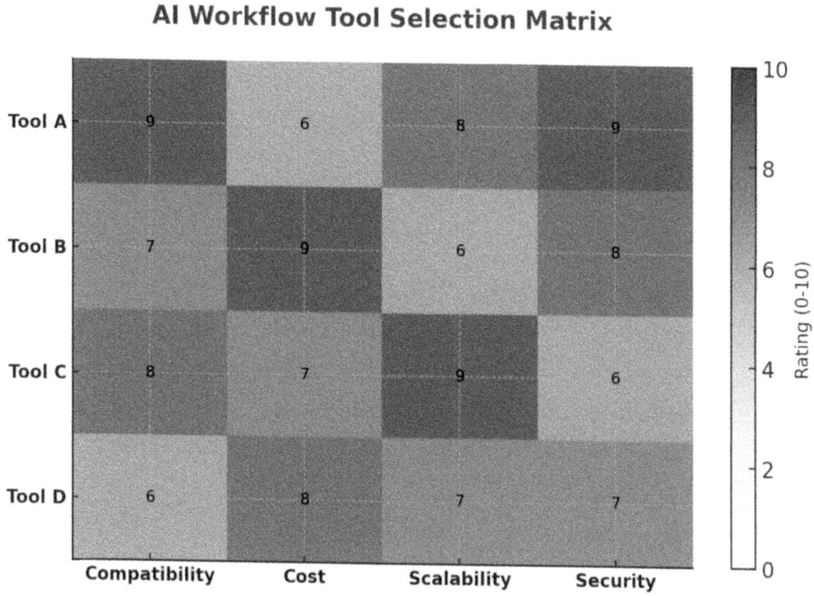

Combining ChatGPT-5 with Other AI Systems

Integrating ChatGPT-5 with other AI systems can greatly expand your capabilities and unlock workflows that go beyond what any single model can achieve on its own. While ChatGPT-5 excels in natural language processing, pairing it with specialized AI tools can result in a more robust and efficient system that addresses diverse needs.

1. Why Combine AI Systems

No single AI model is the best at every task. ChatGPT-5 can generate language, summarize information, and engage in conversation, but image generation, advanced statistical modeling, and real-time speech recognition may be better handled by dedicated models. By combining systems, you can create end-to-end solutions that handle multiple data types and complex workflows seamlessly.

2. Common Pairing Scenarios

- **Text plus Image AI**
  ChatGPT-5 can generate captions, context, or stories for images created by AI image generators such as DALL·E or Stable Diffusion. It can also prepare structured image prompts to improve visual output quality.

- **Text plus Speech AI**
  Integrating ChatGPT-5 with speech-to-text models like Whisper allows real-time transcription of spoken words into text, which ChatGPT-5 can then process, analyze, or enhance before optionally sending it to a text-to-speech system for spoken output.

- **Text plus Data Analytics AI**
  When combined with AI models built for numerical data analysis, ChatGPT-5 can explain complex statistics, prepare natural language summaries of analytical results, and make data insights more accessible.

- **Text plus Search and Knowledge Retrieval**
  Pairing ChatGPT-5 with vector databases or semantic search systems enables access to up-to-date information beyond its training cutoff. This allows responses to incorporate the latest research, news, and domain-specific data.

3. Integration Methods

Combining ChatGPT-5 with other AI systems typically involves API connections, plugins, or a workflow orchestration tool such as Zapier, LangChain, or custom-built pipelines. This integration ensures that data moves smoothly between systems without requiring manual intervention.

4. Benefits of a Multi-AI Workflow

- Broader capability range

- Increased accuracy for specialized tasks
- Enhanced user experience through multimodal interaction
- Reduced workload for each individual AI system, improving speed and reliability

5. Considerations Before Integration

- Ensure compatibility between models and APIs
- Pay attention to latency, as multiple AI calls can increase response times
- Maintain data privacy and security across all integrated systems
- Set clear rules for when each AI takes over specific parts of a task

Why This Matters

Combining ChatGPT-5 with other AI systems is a force multiplier for productivity, creativity, and analytical power. The synergy between different models allows you to design workflows that are tailored to your exact goals while making the most of each AI's unique strengths.

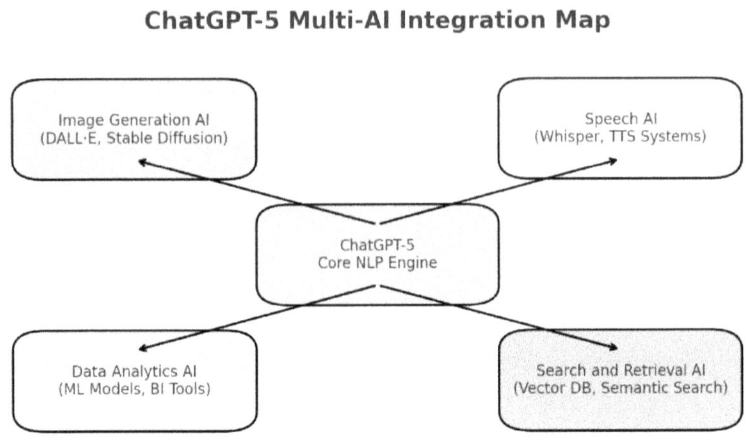

Continuous Learning and Iteration

An effective AI workflow with ChatGPT-5 is not something you set up once and never change. Instead, it is a dynamic process that evolves as your needs shift, technology advances, and you gain new insights into how the system can serve you best. Continuous learning and iteration allow you to refine both the AI's outputs and the way you interact with it, ensuring that your workflow remains efficient, accurate, and aligned with your goals.

1. Adopting a Feedback Loop Mindset

Every interaction with ChatGPT-5 is an opportunity to learn. Whether you receive a perfect output or an incomplete answer, that result gives you information you can use to improve. Build a habit of noting what worked well and what did not, and feed those observations into future prompts, integrations, and processes.

2. Experimenting with Prompt Variations

Small changes in phrasing, context, or role assignment can significantly impact results. By testing variations on a prompt, you can discover patterns that consistently produce higher-quality responses. Keep a record of these findings so you can reuse them.

3. Tracking Performance Over Time
Maintain logs of your AI interactions to measure performance improvements. This could involve qualitative notes, such as "This version provided better detail," or quantitative measures, such as response time or the percentage of answers that required little to no editing.

4. Adapting to New Features
OpenAI regularly updates ChatGPT-5 with new capabilities, plugins, and settings. Staying informed and experimenting with these additions ensures that your workflow benefits from the latest advances.

5. Learning from External Sources
Your improvement process does not have to rely solely on personal trial and error. Study community forums, case studies, and expert articles to see how others are using ChatGPT-5 in similar contexts. Adapt their techniques to your needs.

6. Iterating in Small, Manageable Steps
Instead of attempting to overhaul your workflow all at once, focus on small, targeted changes. This makes it easier to measure the impact of each change and avoid unnecessary complexity.

Why This Matters
A workflow that continuously learns and adapts can keep pace with the evolving nature of AI technology. Iteration is not just about fixing what does not work; it is about proactively seeking better ways to achieve your goals and maintaining a competitive edge in your field.

Continuous Learning and Iteration Feedback Loop

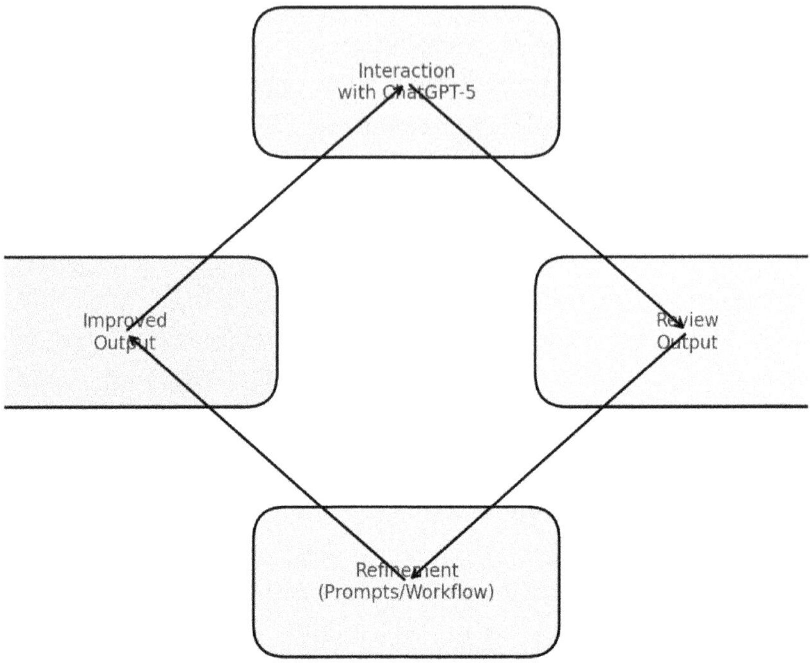

Appendices

Appendix A: Updated Command List and Prompt

This appendix provides an organized reference of the most up-to-date ChatGPT-5 commands, settings, and prompt templates. It serves as a quick-access toolkit for both beginners and experienced users who want to maximize efficiency and consistency in their interactions with the model.

1. Updated Command List

The following is a categorized list of ChatGPT-5's current commands and functions. The actual list may expand over time as new features are introduced.

A. General Interaction Commands

- **/summarize** – Produces a concise summary of the provided text.
- **/expand** – Expands a brief idea into a detailed explanation or full article.
- **/translate [language]** – Translates text into the target language.
- **/rewrite** – Rephrases the text to improve clarity or adjust tone.
- **/explain** – Breaks down complex topics into simpler terms.

B. Creative Content Commands

- **/story** – Generates a short story based on the given theme or prompt.
- **/poem** – Creates poetry using the provided theme, mood, or style.

- **/script** – Produces a dialogue or screenplay segment from given context.
- **/lyrics** – Writes song lyrics in a chosen genre or style.

C. Data and Analytical Commands

- **/analyze** – Evaluates and interprets provided data or text.
- **/compare** – Produces a side-by-side comparison between two or more items.
- **/outline** – Creates a structured outline based on the given topic.
- **/factcheck** – Identifies possible inaccuracies and provides verified facts.

D. Specialized Functional Commands

- **/code** – Generates programming code in a specified language.
- **/debug** – Reviews and suggests fixes for provided code.
- **/api** – Suggests or structures an API request for given functionality.
- **/design** – Produces UI/UX suggestions or wireframe descriptions.

---

2. Prompt Templates

Below are ready-to-use prompt structures that can save time and help maintain clarity.

A. Informational Template

Explain [topic] as if teaching a [beginner/intermediate/advanced] audience. Include [specific examples].

B. Creative Writing Template

Write a [story/poem/script] set in [setting] with a [tone/mood] and [specific character details]. Include a twist at the end.

C. Problem-Solving Template

Given the following problem: [problem statement], list step-by-step reasoning and provide the most practical solution.

D. Comparative Analysis Template

Compare [Item 1] and [Item 2] in terms of [criteria list], and provide a recommendation based on [goal or purpose].

E. Coding Task Template

Write code in [programming language] to perform [functionality], include in-line comments, and suggest possible optimizations.

---

3. How to Use This Appendix

This appendix works best as a quick reference when building prompts or recalling specific ChatGPT-5 capabilities. Users should adapt these templates to their unique needs, adjusting tone, length, and detail level as required.

Appendix B: AI Ethics Guidelines Reference

This appendix serves as a condensed yet comprehensive reference for ethical principles that should guide the development, deployment, and use of ChatGPT-5 and similar AI systems. It consolidates globally recognized AI ethics frameworks and practical recommendations to ensure responsible and transparent AI use.

1. Core Ethical Principles

A. Transparency

AI systems should operate in a way that allows users to understand how outputs are generated. When possible, AI should provide reasoning steps or source references. Clear disclosure that content is AI-generated builds trust and accountability.

B. Fairness and Non-Discrimination

AI should be trained, tested, and monitored to avoid unfair treatment of individuals or groups. Data used in training must be diverse and representative to reduce systemic bias. Any detected bias must be addressed promptly.

C. Privacy and Data Protection

AI interactions should protect user data by avoiding unnecessary storage, anonymizing sensitive information, and complying with regulations such as GDPR. Users should have control over their personal information and the option to delete it.

D. Accountability

There should be a clear assignment of responsibility for AI outputs and their consequences. Human oversight remains essential to ensure decisions align with legal, ethical, and societal norms.

E. Safety and Security

AI systems should be safeguarded against misuse, manipulation, and cyberattacks. This includes both technical security measures and robust monitoring of potential harmful applications.

2. Practical Guidelines for Users of ChatGPT-5

A. Verify Information

Do not assume AI outputs are correct. Always cross-check with credible sources before making important decisions.

B. Use AI as a Support Tool

AI should enhance human decision-making, not replace it entirely. Maintain human oversight for tasks that have significant social, legal, or financial implications.

C. Respect Intellectual Property

Avoid using AI to create or reproduce copyrighted material without permission. When AI contributes to creative work, acknowledge its role appropriately.

D. Avoid Harmful Applications

Do not use AI for activities that could cause harm, spread misinformation, or violate laws. This includes generating malicious content or discriminatory messages.

E. Promote Inclusivity

Design prompts and workflows that reflect diversity in culture, gender, language, and perspective. Inclusivity in AI use can help create outputs that are relevant to broader audiences.

---

3. References to Global Ethical Frameworks

- **OECD AI Principles** – Focus on inclusive growth, human-centered values, transparency, robustness, and accountability.
- **UNESCO AI Ethics Recommendation** – Emphasizes human rights, environmental sustainability, and diversity.
- **EU AI Act Proposals** – Outlines risk-based regulatory approaches for AI deployment.

- **IEEE Ethically Aligned Design** – Provides guidance for integrating ethics into technology development.

Appendix C: Further Reading and Online Resources

This appendix provides a curated collection of books, research papers, articles, and online tools for readers who want to deepen their understanding of ChatGPT-5, AI technologies, prompt engineering, and the ethical and social dimensions of artificial intelligence. These resources are grouped by category to make it easier to find relevant materials.

1. Foundational AI and Machine Learning

Books

- *Artificial Intelligence: A Modern Approach* by Stuart Russell and Peter Norvig – A widely used textbook covering the fundamentals of AI.
- *Deep Learning* by Ian Goodfellow, Yoshua Bengio, and Aaron Courville – A comprehensive introduction to neural networks and deep learning concepts.

Key Articles and Papers

- *Attention Is All You Need* by Vaswani et al. – The original paper introducing the transformer architecture used in models like ChatGPT-5.
- *Language Models are Few-Shot Learners* by Brown et al. – The GPT-3 technical paper explaining the scaling and prompt-based learning approach.

Online Resources

- Coursera's *Machine Learning* course by Andrew Ng.
- MIT OpenCourseWare's *Deep Learning for Self-Driving Cars* (also relevant for understanding neural networks).

2. ChatGPT-Specific Learning

Guides and Tutorials

- OpenAI's official documentation and help center.
- Prompt engineering tutorials from reputable AI blogs such as Towards Data Science.

Communities

- OpenAI Community Forum – A place to share prompts, ask questions, and discuss use cases.
- Reddit's r/ChatGPT – A user-driven hub for sharing experiences and creative ideas.

---

3. Ethics, Policy, and Social Impact

Books

- *Weapons of Math Destruction* by Cathy O'Neil – An exploration of bias and inequality in algorithmic decision-making.
- *The Ethical Algorithm* by Michael Kearns and Aaron Roth – How to design algorithms that are both useful and fair.

Papers and Reports

- UNESCO's *Recommendation on the Ethics of Artificial Intelligence.*
- The OECD AI Principles.

Websites

- Partnership on AI – Research and best practices for responsible AI.
- AI Now Institute – Reports on the social implications of AI technologies.

4. Practical Tools and Experimentation Platforms

- OpenAI Playground – Experiment with ChatGPT-5 in a customizable environment.
- Hugging Face – Access a variety of open-source transformer models for experimentation.
- Google Colab – Run Python code and AI experiments in the cloud for free.

---

5. Keeping Up with AI Developments

- AI research newsletters such as *The Batch* by deeplearning.ai.
- AI news sites like VentureBeat AI and Synced Review.
- Follow AI researchers on platforms like Twitter and LinkedIn to get real-time updates on breakthroughs.

www.ingramcontent.com/pod-product-compliance
Ingram Content Group UK Ltd.
Pitfield, Milton Keynes, MK11 3LW, UK
UKHW020124290926
15471UKWH00003B/273

9 798868 909542